I.S.B.N. : 2-7118-2285-0 (2e édition revue et corrigée)
(I.S.B.N. : 2-7118-0189-6 1re édition)

Malmaison

by
Gérard Hubert

Curator-in-chief
of the National Museum
of the Château of Malmaison

Translation : C. de Chabannes

Ministère de la Culture, de la Communication,
des Grands Travaux et du Bicentenaire

Editions de la Réunion des musées nationaux,
Paris 1989

Cover :

1
The Château : detail of the façades overlooking
the main courtyourd on the East (17th and late 18th centuries).

Malmaison day by day

Malmaison before Josephine

Josephine's Malmaison

Malmaison after Josephine

The history of Malmaison before Josephine takes into account the discoveries of M. Bernard Chevallier, curator. He had drawn up the list of known owners since its origins and made drawings of their coats-of-arms.

2
General view of the Malmaison gardens, about 1808. Engraving by de Saulx from Constant Bourgeois. In the background, the Temple of Love and on the right the hot-house. In the distance, the aqueduct of Marly.

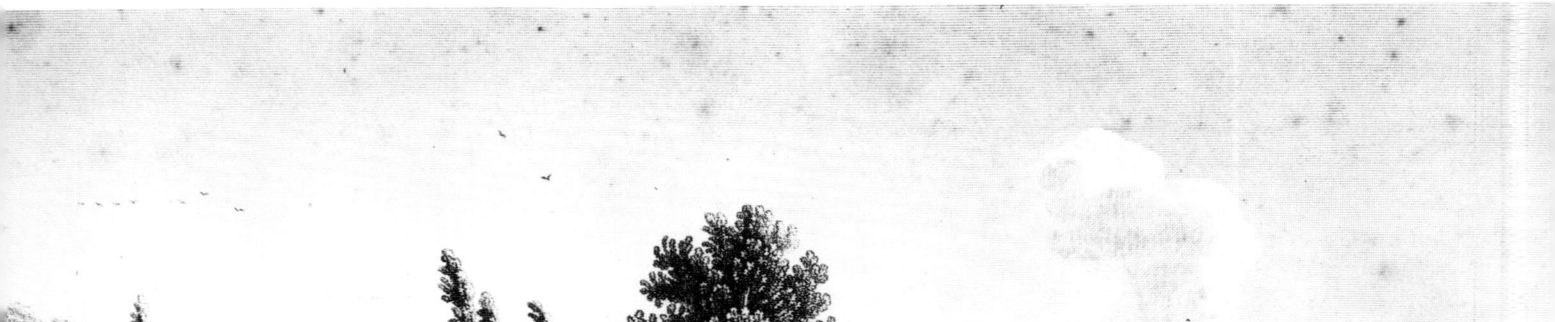

Malmaison before Josephine

Ever since prehistoric times, man has left his mark on the site of Rueil, close by the banks of the Seine, some fifteen kilometres west of the place which was to become Paris. The name of Rueil is mentioned for the first time about the year 550, as that of a royal residence where Childebert, son of Clovis, stayed among others. In 840, the Normans sailed up the Seine in their drakkars and disembarked not far from there. Charles the Bald tried in vain to dislodge them from Bougival and the site of Malmaison, which they devastated, but these plunderers disappeared fairly soon. In the Spring of 875, the castellany of Rueil was presented by the same sovereign to the Abbey of St. Denis. The feudal ties thus established were to last till the end of the 17th century, long after the abbots had divided up and transferred their property. The acts of "recognition and enumeration" furnished by the vassals to their suzerain at each mutation have luckily been preserved, as have those of "faith and homage" drawn up at the election of each new abbot, and these, like the less ancient titles to the property, make it possible to follow the fate of the domain without discontinuity throughout the Middle Ages. The barn of Malmaison is not mentioned till September 1244. At the beginning of the following century, it belonged to Onfroy de Carépatrie (or Kirk Patrick) d'Estor, of Scottish birth, described as a bourgeois of Paris. He had no heir and presented it about 1330 to Abbot Guy de Châtres, his suzerain, who gave it in his turn in 1339 to the Bureau of Charities of Saint-Denis. The domain was reassigned two years later to an important personnage, Robert de Lorris, clerk and councillor to the King, brother-in-law of Etienne Marcel, the future provost of the Merchants of Paris.

MEULAN
about 1200

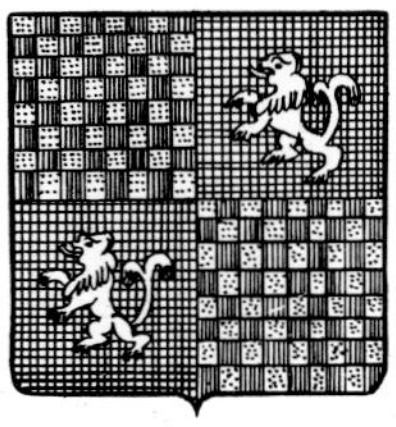

SAINT DENIS
1330-1341

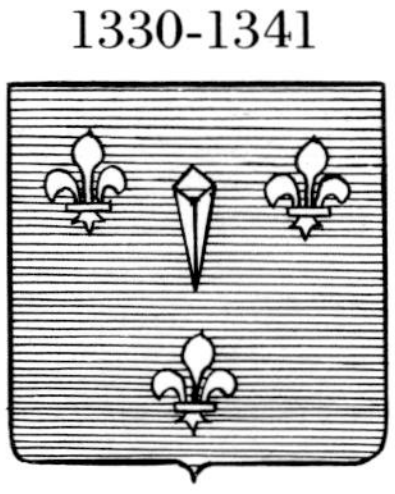

LORRIS
1341 - before 1362

It was ravaged in 1346 by the bands ot the Black Prince, son of Edward III, during the so-called Hundred years War between France and England. Its new owner, Agnès, countess of Acquise, widow of Thomas de la Marche, a bastard of Philip VI of Valois, swore faith and homage to the Abbey in 1362, but quickly resold it to Nicolas de Chevreuse, the King's bailiff-at-arms, who soon ceded the Malmaison to the Chevalier Guy de Gouy. His recognition in 1376, reveals the existence of a manorhouse, with courtyard, farmyard, ploughing-fields and vineyards yielding good profits.

LA MARCHE
about 1362

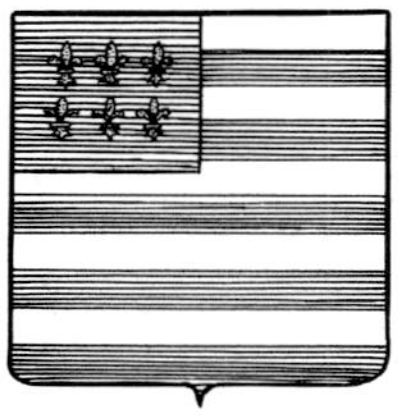

When Guillaume Goudet, a Parisian merchant and royal Sergeant-at-arms, acquired the Malmaison in 1346, it passed at last to a family which was to keep it for nearly four centuries, until 1763. The only change is in the names of its owners, on account of numerous successions by the female line. For instance: Agnès Goudet married Jean Dubois, lawyer at the Châtelet in Paris, a partisan of the Burgundians and thus of the English. Marie, daughter of Agnès and Jean Dubois, married Jean Dauvergne, who became Master of Butchers in Paris. When the Armagnacs entered Paris, the Malmaison was confiscated and the Abbot of Saint-Denis entrusted with its administration in 1414. Jean Dauvergne regained it; his son Hugues, then his grandson Claude remained in possession till the death of the latter in 1561 or 1562. His daughter Marie, wife of Jean Perrot, left the domain in 1563 to her grandson Claude Perrot, lord of the Malmaison, who became President of the Court of Enquiry of the Châlons Parliament. Mention of the old 14th century manor can be found only in the archives.

DAUVERGNE
about 1420-1561

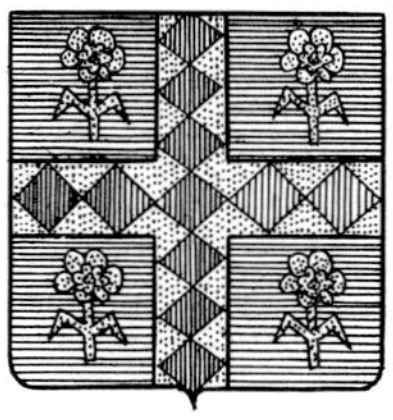

Christophe Perrot, son of the "President" and himself a councillor to the Paris Parliament, took possession in 1597 and started at the beginning of the 17th century to reconstruct the main building, which had doubtless been damaged during the wars of Religion which had raged around Rueil. He died in 1641. At that time the Malmaison could not compare with the splendid residence fitted up by Jacques Lemercier for Cardinal Richelieu at the entrance to Rueil, which became its real castle but which disappeared during the 19th century.

It was in fact a mere manor, the centre of a large agricultural estate. The dwelling-house faced North and South and comprised at that time a very simple building with two storeys of unequal height and nine windows opening on the courtyard to the East and the garden to the West, flanked on the South by a pavilion with a high slated roof. There is no trace of pilasters, columns, decorated doors or exterior sculptures. The few rooms are of fair size and overlook both the courtyard and the garden. The windows of the kitchens, cellars and store-rooms in the basement give onto a sunk fence on the West. The Perrots lived less in the Malmaison than in Paris, where they did their business.

PERROT
1561-1713

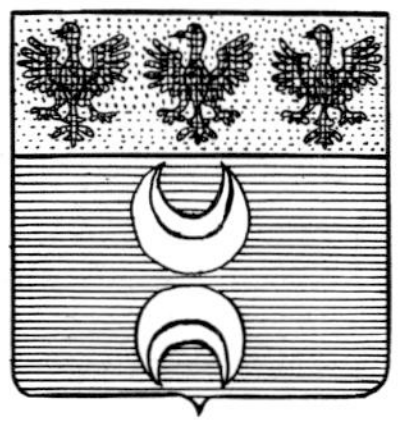

Charles, son of Christophe Perrot, succeeded his father and died in 1685. One of his daughters married Jacques-Honoré Barentin, first President of the Grand Council, and the domain passed to her.

President Barentin then decided to complete the work begun half a century earlier. In 1686, he built the North Pavilion and the small mansard-roofed wing adjoining it; in the following year, he added an identical building to the South Pavilion and built the great stairway of the castle up against it. The work was carried out by two master-masons of Rueil, Laurent and Jean Vase. The apartments are arranged as they were during the whole of the 18th century: the drawing-rooms occupy the large and the small North pavilions, after which one came, just as one does today, to a billiard-room, a hall and a dining-room. The two South pavilions contain the apartments of Madame on the ground-floor and those of Monsieur on the first floor.

The Barentins, however, were given positions in the provinces and lost interest in this property, which they leased out with the farms. Gerard Michel, lord of La Jonchère, and his wife Charlotte Raisin, natural daughter of the Grand Dauphin, became life-tenants in 1737 and during the next two years carried out important transformations in the decoration of the apartments. Blue or daffodil-yellow panellings were enriched by mirrors and dessus-de-portes; all the rooms were fitted up with alcoves and wardrobe-cabinets, while the furniture of the reception rooms was completely renewed. The park was marked out afresh, while the natural slope of the stream was used to create numerous water-pieces of which only the names remain: the Louis XV waterfall, the Etrennes fountain, etc.

After the death of M. de La Jonchère, his widow who, according to the Duc de Luynes "did not like the country", sub-let to Guillaume-Paul Tavernier de Boulogne, who invited the Controllor-General of Finance, Moreau de Séchelles, to spend his convalescence in the château in 1756. After the death of Madame de La Jonchère in 1757, M. Barentin renewed the lease in favour of M. de Boulogne, who sub-let in his turn in about 1760 to an important Farmer-General, Jacques Verdeilhan, seigneur des Fourniels, and his wife. The couple entertained a select society, among which was witty Madame Harenc, a great friend of Madame du Deffand, and the poet Marmontel who wrote some of his stories among this set which was at once homelike and worldly, "beside the brook of Malmaison which flows down a steep slope from the top of the hill and winds along, under bowers of greenery to groove the flowery lawns."

The Barentins finally found a buyer on May 4th 1763, in the person of Henri d'Aguesseau, State Councillor, eldest son of the Chancellor. He died, however, in the following year and his widow hastened to sell the domain on March 23rd 1771, for 180,000 pounds to Jacques-Jean Le Couteulx du Moley. The latter was a member of a family of Normandy financiers, Receiver-General of the Lottery and administrator of the Discount Bank. He had married in 1769 his first cousin, Sophie Le Couteulx de la Noraye, whose brother Laurent owned the château of Voisins, at Louveciennes. The new proprietors made numerous alterations and partially transformed the gardens in the English style, building a tower containing a natural history collection. For the apartments, they chiefly ordered the mahogany furniture fashionable at the time. The two short wings prolonging the pavilions in the direction of the courtyard also seem to have been built at this time. They gave brilliant receptions to which

BARENTIN
1713-1763

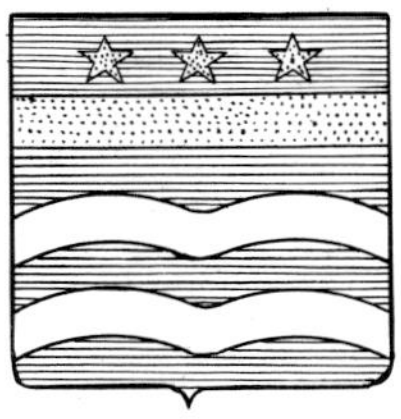

DAGUESSEAU
1763-1764

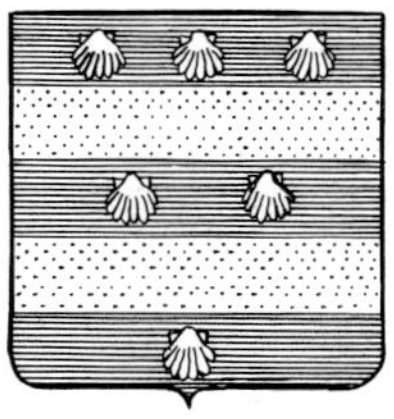

3
Plan of the château and park, about 1740, from a topographical map of the Paris region drawn up by Abbé Delagrive.

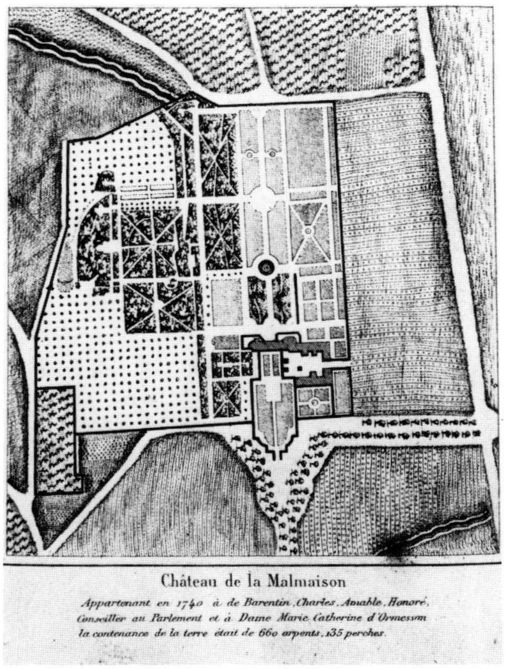

NOLLENT
1764-1771

LE COUTEULX DU MOLAY
1771-1799

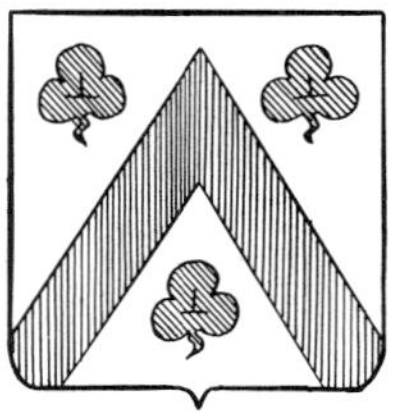

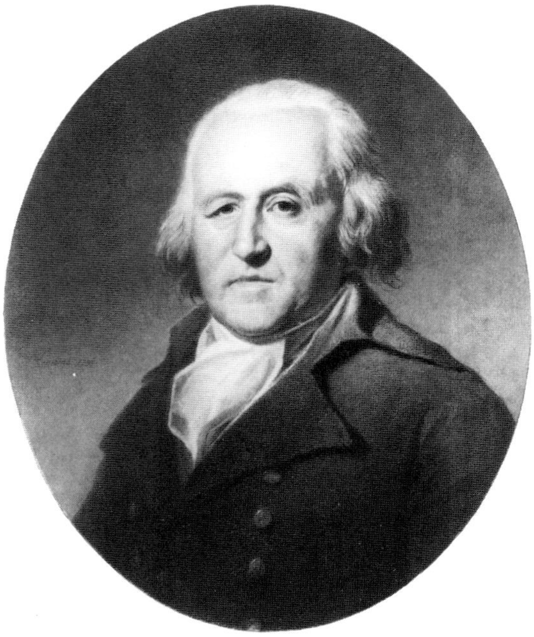

4
Jacques-Jean Le Couteulx du Moley in 1796.
Rubbed charcoal drawing, signed Lemoine
(presumably Jacques-Antoine Marie, 1751-1824) and dated.

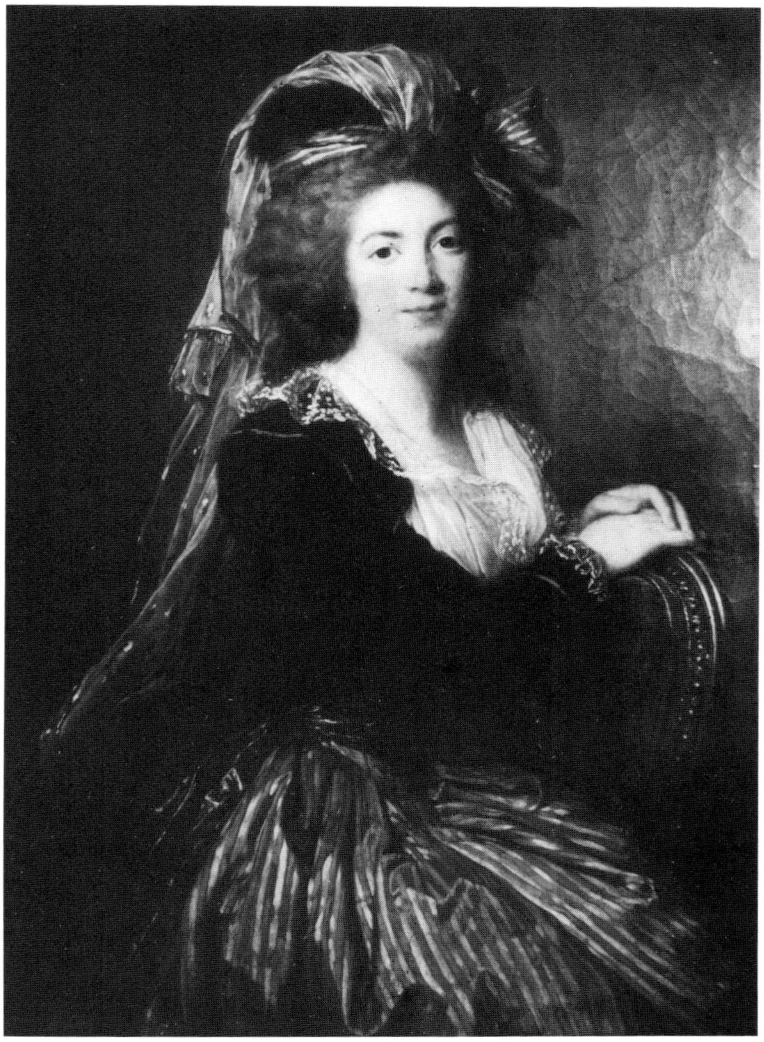

5
Sophie Le Couteulx, portrait
painted by Madame Vigée-Lebrun
in 1788 (Paris, Nissim de Camondo Museum).

came an élite of nobles, artists, poets an philosophers, such as the duc de Crillon, the comte Olivares, in whose honour a steep path was baptised "Sierra Morena", Suard, the abbé Morellet, Choderlos de Laclos, who had just published *Les Liaisons Dangereuses*, the baron de Grimm, always on the lookout for a bit of gossip, the American Governor Morriss, Bernardin de Saint-Pierre, the Italian poet Alfieri and the comtesse d'Albany, André Chénier, a close friend of the La Norayes, the brothers de Pange, Pauline de Beaumont and her brother Antoine de La Luzerne, Condorcet, the abbé Siéyès, Barthélemy Le Couteulx de Canteleu, Bonaparte's future banker. A frequent visitor was the abbé Delille, Sophie's favourite poet, translator of the *Georgics* and author of *Les Jardins*, in which he evokes "the Malmaison, so pleasant with its beautiful woods, water-pieces, views and position". In his *Correspondance*, Grimm copies Sophie's character-portrait of him: "... his mind is fifteen years old, so it is easy to know. It is affectionate and goes in twenty directions all at once... He pays attention to one's conversation, it's true, but he may just as well spend a couple of hours stroking his horse, which he nevertheless sometimes forgets, or wandering in the woods where, when he is not afraid, he dreams of the moon, or a blade of grass, or rather, of his own dreams He is Platon's poet, a sacred being, flighty and fickle." Delille published "The brook at Malmaison" in his *Pièces fugitives*, "verses for Madame du Moley's feast-day", with their false naiveté:

> Among the pleasures prepared for you,
> Permit, sweet Eglé, the god of the brook
> Who, charmed to bathe your pleasant retreat,
> Oft sees you dreaming to the soft sound of his water,
> To join this happy fête.

The comparison with the waterfalls and pools of Marly naturally favours the "brook".

Madame Vigée-Lebrun, Marie-Antoinette's favourite portraitist, was happy to meet "dear Abbé Delille who often came to Malmaison. Mme du Moley liked to walk alone and I entirely shared this taste... It was understood that if one held a branch of greenery in one's hand, one did not want to meet people or talk. I never walked without my branch; but if I saw the Abbé Delille, I quickly threw it away". However, she judged her hostess severely: "Mme du Moley was a pretty woman who was much in fashion; her own mind was not quick, but she understood other peoples' intelligently". Her memories were not always rustic. "In June 1789, I went to dine at Malmaison and found there the Abbé Siéyès and several others favourable to the Revolution. M. du Moley screamed against the nobility... it was just like being in a club and these conversations frightened me horribly. After dinner Abbé Siéyès said to someone: "I really think we go too far." "They will go so far that they will get lost on the way," I said to Mme du Moley, who had also heard the abbé and was saddened by all these sinister forebodings."

In spite of his advanced ideas, Le Couteulx tried to save the King by giving a large sum to the Spanish ambassador in the hope that he could arrange for Louis XVI to be judged by an elected national jury and not by the Convention. He was imprisoned, deep in debt, and the couple was forced to sell Malmaison.

6
Abbé Delille in 1777. Engraving by Vangelisty from A. Pujos.

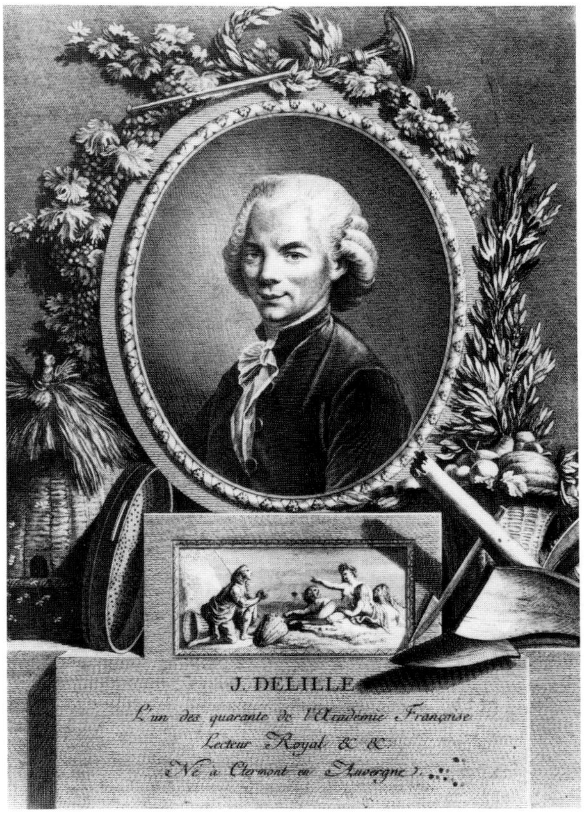

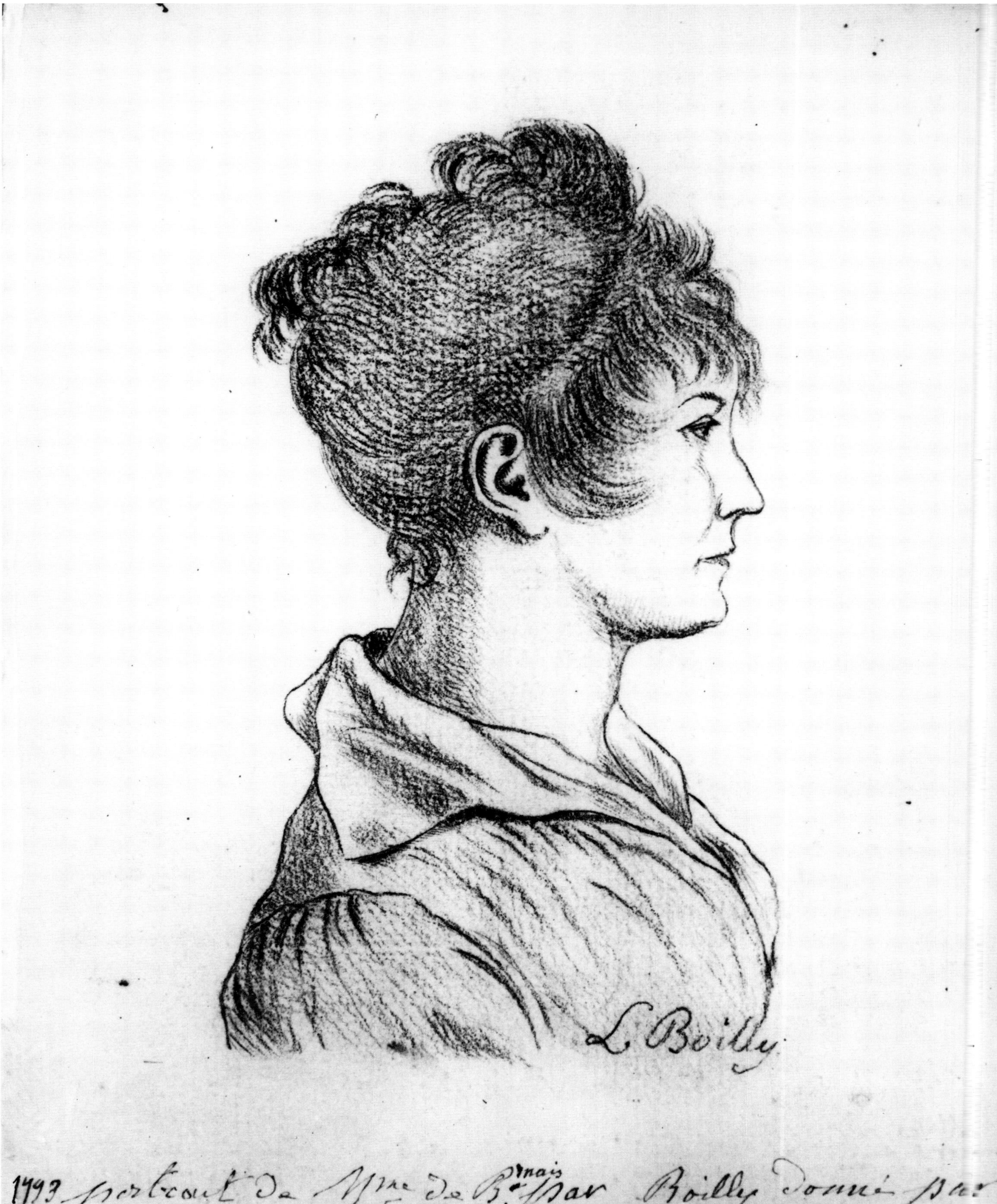

7
Madame de Beauharnais in 1793, drawing by Boilly, presented by Queen Hortense to Valérie Mazuyer en 1834
(gift of Comte d'Esdouhard).

Josephine's Malmaison

The purchase of Malmaison

At this point there comes into the story a Creole from Martinique, already preparing for a dazzling destiny and who was to bring unexpected prestige to the Malmaison. Marie-Joseph-Rose de Tascher de la Pagerie was born on June 23rd 1763, at Trois-Ilets, of an ancient and sufficiently noble family from the province of Perche. She had made a very early marriage to Alexandre de Beauharnais – a marriage of convenience which turned out unhappily in spite of the birth of two children, Eugène and Hortense. By the start of the Revolution, the couple had obtained a separation, with the husband as the guilty party. Alexandre was an officer; he threw himself into militant politics, presided over the Constituent Assembly, even commanded the Rhine Army for a time, then was arrested, while the Vicomtesse de Beauharnais sought refuge at Croissy with her friend Mme Hosten, widow of J.-B. de Lamothe-Hosten. From Croissy, where her son Eugène was apprenticed to the carpenter Cochard, she could see the roofs of Malmaison and dream of being its landowner. She was imprisoned in her turn and met General de Beauharnais again at the prison of Les Carmes. He was condemned and guillotined on July 23rd 1794, while she was liberated on August 6th after the fall of Robespierre. Widowed and pennyless she returned to Croissy, where she became friendly again with Chanorier, once the lord and now the first mayor of the village. She was fascinating, she belonged to the dissipated set of "les Merveilleuses", she was a friend of Barras. Thus she won the heart of the young Corsican general Bonaparte, who was much in the limelight since the

TASCHER DE LA PAGERIE
1799-1814

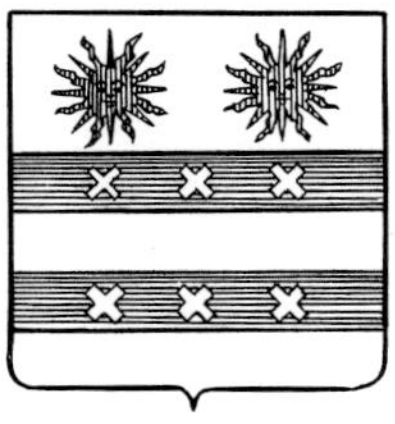

BEAUHARNAIS
1814-1824

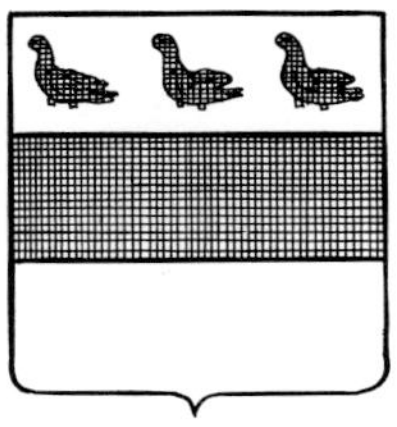

retaking of Toulon and the successful outcome of the day of 13 Vendémiaire. The marriage took place on March 9th, 1796 and immediately after Bonaparte was appointed commander of the army in Italy, which he was to lead from victory to victory. The hero was a rich man now and he desired to possess a country seat where he could escape from the traps set for him in a Paris of which he was not yet entirely the master. "Having heard of this, Madame Le Couteulx, with whom I was on friendly terms", recounts Isabey (at that time drawing-master at Madame Campan's academy, where young Hortense was his best pupil) "asked me to approach Madame Bonaparte on the subject of a property she owned near Rueil. Madame Bonaparte consented to visit it; I accompanied her and the transaction was carried out on the spot". In reality, the negociations hung fire, since Bonaparte thought the price too high, and he was also detained by preparations for the Egyptian expedition. During the next Spring, while he was vainly besieging St.-Jean d'Acre, Josephine made up her mind on the advice of Chanorier. A long letter from the latter, dated 11 ventôse, year VII (March Ist, 1799) is worth quoting, at least in part, for the details it contains:

8
Sabre worn by General Bonaparte at Arcole.

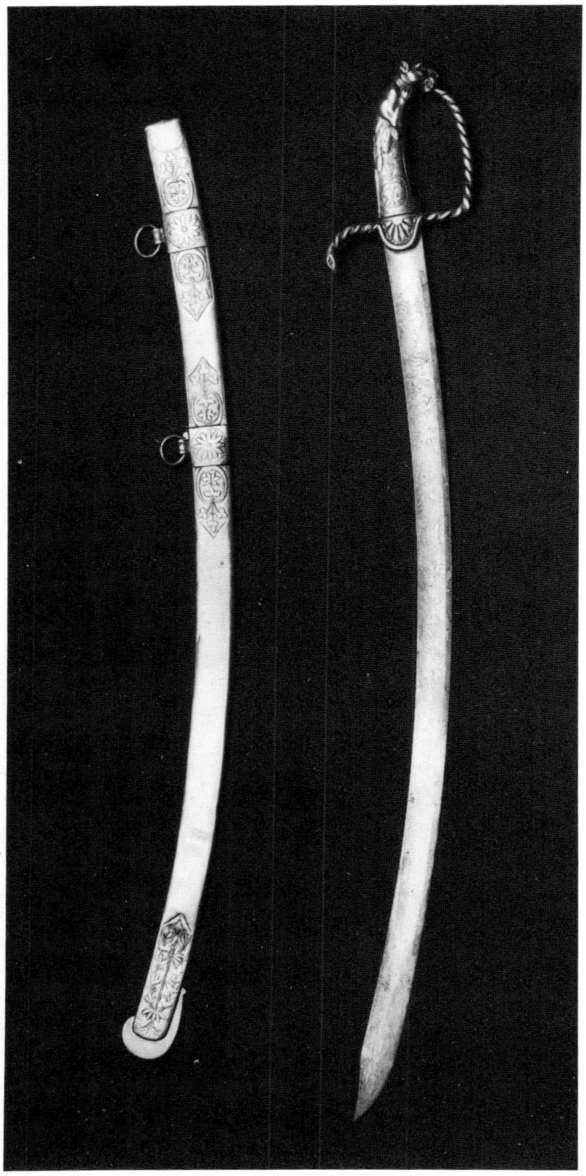

"This morning, my dear neighbour, I spent four hours at Malmaison, where I found Mme du Moley... If you were as rich as is generally believed, I would speak only of the advantages of the prettiest property I know, but you need to make a useful acquisition and the Malmaison is such a one... Mme du Moley began by showing me a letter offering her 200,000 francs down and a national domain bringing in 11,000 francs in rent for the Malmaison without the furniture... I asked for her final proposal." 300,000 francs" she replied. General Bonaparte offered them to my relative, the representant Canteleux, who is ready to swear to it. That was a month after he took his walk at Malmaison." I repeated that the general had only told you of an offer of 250,000 francs; but supposing that he had later offered 300,000, the value of the land has gone down since then and I should like to bring you a more acceptable proposition: I said that 300,000 for the grounds, about 25,000 for the furniture, 150,000 for the agricultural furnishings, the provisions in the attics to be acquired... and about 15,000 francs in duties to be paid to the nation, would mean that you would have to put down about 360,000 francs. Thus I asked Mme du Moley to speak to her husband, who was in the house, but disliked discussing the sale of lands he had so much improved and embellished, and had begged her to receive me and ask for my final offer. She went to fetch him and during this time I visited all the properties with the guardian."

"A two-hours walk and a long conversation procured the following details... These lands have been committed to a steward for the last thirty years... He says there are 387 arpents of wheat, vines, woods and meadows. The grounds are excellent. This year, they made 120 barrels of wine selling at 50 francs. Twenty-five people live on M. du Moley's estate and the farm people all live without buying anything... If the land-value had not gone down, Malmaison should sell for 500,000 francs."

Chanorier calculated the income Josephine would draw from

the estate... "apart from the park which counts 75 arpents and contains woods, vines and meadows, there would remain 312 arpents for letting, and by renting them at only 30 francs, tax-free, this would amount to 9,360, and adding to this the income from the park, estimated at 6,000, but which I reduce to 3,000, this would bring in a total income of 12,000. This should reassure you."

"I rejoined Mme du Moley and she told me her husband's final word. He wants 290,000 francs for the "ci-devant" château, the mirrors he estimates at 20,000, the agricultural furnishings, 7 horses, 12 cows, 150 sheep, pigs and the farm-yard animals... Thus I have persuaded him to make several sacrifices, first of all 10,000 and the agricultural furnishings which are worth at least 12 to 15,000. Mme du Moley will sell the furniture according to the estimate of two upholsterers... and she will let you know the few objects she wishes to keep... He wants... 150,000 down and 50,000 francs afterwards. This does not carry the payments beyond the periods you desired, Madame. The surplus will be paid a year later..."

9
The château of the Malmaison, on the garden side. Engraving by Perdoux from Constant Bourgeois.

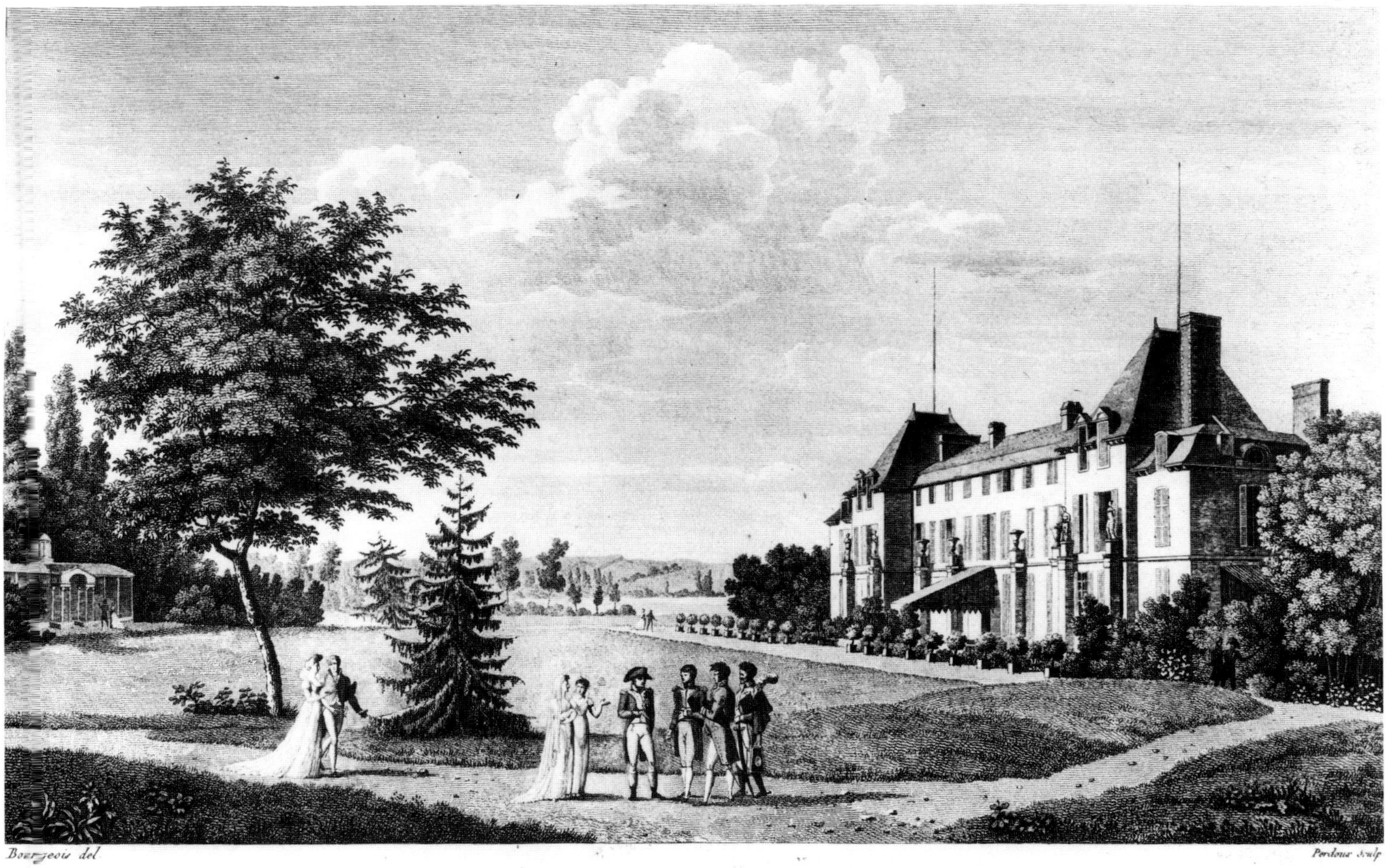

Bourgeois del — Perdoux Sculp

Le CHÂTEAU de la MALMAISON, du côté des Jardins.

"I must tell you that poor Mme du Moley trembled when I told her you were tired of Paris and that if you make the purchase you may possibly settle in a fortnight later. She intended to stay there a long time in the summer. I must also tell you that she and her husband occupy a charming apartment in the farmhouse, separated from the château in which there are said to be twenty apartments. She asked if it would inconvenience you to leave her there until Thermidor... Then you could settle into the château the day after the purchase and in this way you would be on even better terms with the guardian, whom you will need till the lease is drawn up."

"I forgot to tell you that 300 woolly-coated animals can be kept at Malmaison and that this could add to the income from the land. The property is the most practical and pleasant I have yet seen. But I repeat that its sole income might be insufficient since the house is large and the farmhouse splendid. The latter is amazing."

"Goodbye, my dear neighbour, how happy I shall be if this purchase, with its practical advantages, adds charm to your life."

It was hard to resist such enthusiasm. Josephine did not hesitate, in spite of the uncertainty of her own position, in the absence of a husband whom she knew to have been informed of her conduct and prepared to divorce her. She merely got the lawyer to change the dates of the two payments planned, a fact which brought her at least two letters in which Sophie Le Couteulx expressed her anxiety on March 27th and 29th. Josephine was "separated concerning property" from her husband and on 2 floréal year VII (April 21st 1799) she personally acquired in the presence of her lawyer, Me Raguideau, the domain comprising 260 hectares of good land, the château, its outbuildings, including the nine rooms of the "Clock Building", the four-storeyed tower with its "Natural History Cabinet", the "Pavilion of Liberty", the orangery, the hothouse, the press-house, the dovecot, the mill and the "lodging of the citizen Lhuillier", the guardian. "The present sale is for the sum of 225,000 francs... of which price the purchaser... has now paid... the sum of 15,000 francs... The Ctn Bonaparte states that the 15,000 francs just paid come from a loan to Jean Lhuillier, farmer at Rueil." The latter, "coarsely cunning" according to the architect Fontaine, continued to act as steward and the "complete reimbursement and interests of the sum in question" were not repaid till December 1810. The furniture, estimated at 37,516.65 francs was paid for separately.

10
General Bonaparte, portrait made in Milan by Bacler d'Albe, head of the Ordnance Survey, in the year V (end 1796 or early 1797) (gift Chefdebien).

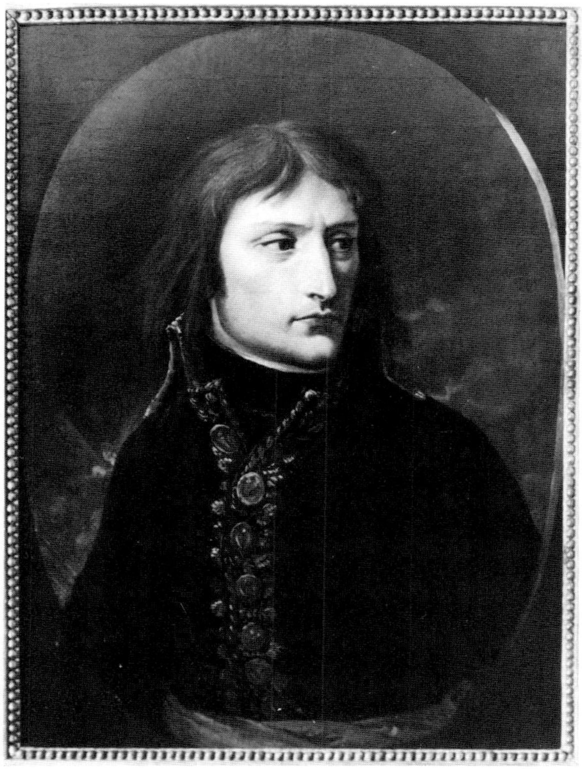

The transfer taxes amounted to 9,111.68 francs. Josephine admitted in a letter to Chanorier that the total price came well up to 325,000 francs. She settled in immediately, in company with Hippolyte Charles, her associate in the transactions of the Co. Bodin, whose puns greatly amsed her and whom the people of Rueil took to be her brother. She organized a housewarming party without worrying about her debt.

The general returned unexpectedly in October and she was forgiven. He became first Consul of the Republic by the coup d'Etat of 18-19 brumaire year VIII (9-10 November 1799) and instructed Me Raguideau on 21 frimaire to pay "for him and in his name" the sums owing for Malmaison. He sent for the lawyer on 29 frimaire (20 December) doubtless in order to sign the arrangement by which he became the veritable owner of Malmaison. He had the good taste to renounce his rights immediately after the divorce.

Now Malmaison makes its entry into history. Bonaparte was happy there, far from the "drudgery" and the sinister Palace of the Tuileries. He protested bitterly against the excessive cost of modernizing the apartments, altering the park and the extra grounds which Josephine had insisted on buying, but he paid. He was to be seen at Malmaison every ten days, sometimes for several days at a time. After his official winter and summer residences at the Tuileries and Saint-Cloud, Napoléon spent in all ten months and twelve days at Malmaison, much longer than at Fontainebleau, Compiègne, Trianon or Rambouillet.

Malmaison under the consulate

Fontaine, with the modest and efficient Percier as his assistant, was entrusted with the modernization of the old mansion and to him we owe the precious journal of the work carried out during the most brilliant and animated years of Malmaison. The two friends would have liked to build a new château on the slope of the hill and they drew up plans in the classic style: the old building (preserved and doubled in size) was to have sheltered the outhouses. Bonaparte would have none of it: "...we have to rebuild a badly constructed house, which is falling into ruin and was made for a very ordinary sort of person."

The Consul had no patience with his architects: the "vestibule in the form of a tent, where we meant the servants to stay in front of the salons...on the side of the entrance, seemed to him like a cage for animals to be shown at a fair", probably because of the bars protecting the panes of this verandah. The two poles terminating in a globe and a gilded crescent, framing an ornamental pediment decorated with a panoply of weapons, must have reminded him of Egypt. This curious pavilion, with its military aspect, preceded a vast, well-lit room opening onto both the courtyard and the garden, its ceiling supported by four stucco columns, its walls painted in imitation marble, porphyry and granite, and decorated with Roman designs in partly gilded relief, swords and crowns of laurel. Fontaine notes on May 5th 1800: "We mean the ground floor to open by arcades... and to use moving mirrors, with or without silvering, so as to make, so to speak, a single room out of the three forming the main building between the two pavilions." The billiard-room adjoining on the North, also served as a salon for the ladies and officers. Then came an unpretentious vestibule opening on to the North stairway and the salon. On July 20th, Fontaine noted: "The new decoration for the salon, executed in ten days by the citizens Jacob, is not as successful as the small gallery and the billard-room. The all-mahogany wainscotting, the velvet framing and the draperies over the doors give a gloomy effect. We asked for two large paintings from the citizens Girodet and Gérard, and four small ones from the citizens Bidault, Taunay, Dunouy and Thibault to fill the panels between the pilasters. Mme Bonaparte desired to have paintings representing scenes from the general's life." Bonaparte was enthusiastic over the strange, romantic compositions of Gérard and Girodet, who had found their inspiration in the poems of Ossian, but he soon caused the other paintings to be taken down.

By March 22nd 1800, "the decoration of the small gallery... excuted by the citizens Jacob and Moench, has been completed and placed in position in ten days. This work had a great success and the First Consul, who is said to be difficult to satisfy,appeared to be pleased with it."

The architects had a good deal of trouble with the dining-room on the South. On March 22nd, Bonaparte "ordered that the dining-room should be enlarged and all the small rooms preceding the bedchamber pulled down; that an apartment should be made for him in the North Pavilion, above the drawing-room... On May 5th, "the are demolishing the rooms between the dining-room and the bed-chamber"; a rotten beam on the upper floor and a whole bay will have to be replaced. The piers on the façade are in a very bad state. Finally we decided to place the beam on upright wooden posts on both fronts of the interior." These can still be seen by the start of the hemicycle part of this room with its charming decoration of Pompeian dancers painted on stucco. "In order to carry out this work, the whole ceiling of the dining-room must be reconstructed. We build in the cellars under two stoves, the hot-air vents and pipes of which will heat the room." This room no longer in fact had any fireplace but only a fountain, the canalizations of which still exist in the wall. The statue which poured water into the basin is known only through a sketch and a mention in the inventory.

July 9th, after the victory of Marengo, "the dining-room, billiard-room and vestibule are nearly finished. The First Consul, who is back again, is pleased with the changes; he has ordered the drawing-room to be decorated, and a council-chamber to replace his bedchamber on the ground-floor, and a library in the corner pavilion leading from it on the South side; he will have his rooms on the first floor, above the reception-room."

August 8th, "we are making a bathroom on the first floor near the First Consul's bedchamber, on the side of the entrance; a toilet cabinet, a small bedroom and smaller rooms on the other side above the gallery." These details, completed by later documents, have made it possible to do away with the clumsy restoratiom of the boudoir transformed into a bathroom. It overlooked the park on the West and was situated South of the bedchamber. The latter was at that time rectangular and contained a safe concealed in the wall. It was brightened by an amusing painted fresco with antique and modern motifs, including scientific instruments — among them an electrical machine. These are now covered over with draperies. "In spite of the French fashion of separate rooms, the

First Consul and his wife sleep under the same canopy", remarked Sir John Carr, who visited France after the Peace of Amiens. Nevertheless Bonaparte often used the corner room, communicating with that of Josephine.

August 26th, "we are hard at work rebuilding the walls of the South wing... and preparing the library and the council-chamber." In their *Recueil de décorations intérieures*, Percier and Fontaine publish the engraving, with the comment: "... it seems suitable to adopt... the form of a tent supported by pikes, fasces and standards, between which hang trophies of weapons recalling those used by the most famous warlike peoples in the world." This tent was of striped twill and was erected in ten days.

"The library.. presents great difficulties, including that of keeping the kitchen chimney-pipe, which is beneath it and cannot be put anywhere else." An ingenious solution was found: the two elements with small mahogany columns joined by the arch nearest the Consul's desk were garnished with mirrors, thus forming a sort of recess without spoiling the original composition of the ensemble.

September 18th, "M. Jacob who has been entrusted with the cabinet-making and carpentry of the library... has worked in an exceptionally intelligent way... Everything is in place now, and though the First Consul thought this room looked like the sacristy of a church, he was obliged to admit that it would have been hard to do better with such unsuitable premises; it remains for us to paint the ceiling..." Percier provided the drawings of the couple Minerva-Apollo in the centre, the medallions of writers and thinkers throughout the ages, without forgetting Bonaparte's favourite Ossian, and flowered trellises gracefully ornamenting the culs-de-four on the East and West, executed by the specialist Moench. By September 27th, "the painters have finished decorating the ceilings of the library and painting the fresco around the First Consul's bedchamber, on the first floor, over the drawing-room."

However, "the façade of the house is in a very bad state, having been seriously damaged by the construction of the vestibule, the dining-room and then the Council-chamber; so that we are obliged to raise stone buttresses on the exterior, between the windows. This will not spoil the façades, which are not at all extraordinary. These buttresses, in any case, will carry statues or vases and will form some sort of decoration for this graceless house." Alexandre Lenoir, director of the Museum of French Monuments, and the directors of the Central Museum of Arts in the Louvre lost no time in sending decorative sculptures, which have since been dispersed.

December 10th, "we are still arranging the interior of Malmaison, finishing the First Consul's apartment and the construction of two small staircases, one leading down from his bedchamber to the Gallery (since demolished) and the other leading from the first floor to the library and the council-chamber (still in existence). We regret that the former situation of the house and the successive changes executed up to the present day prevent us from constructing the First Consul's apartment and his library one above the other. It results from the present arrangement that the First

11
The stone bridge leading to the park, with the obelisks set up in 1807 and the statues of centaurs (modern bronzes, copied from the antique) restored to their original places.

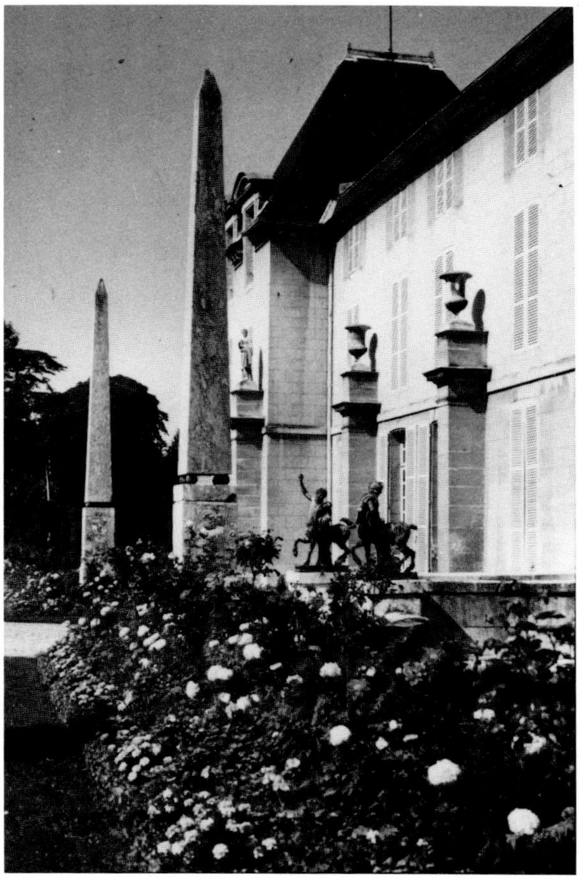

Consul is obliged to go through the whole length of the house when he leaves his bedchamber for the study or the council-chamber. He must either pass by the corridor on the first floor, or go down into the gallery and cross through the rooms on the ground floor."

Napoleon soon changed his bedchamber for a smaller apartment over the council-chamber and the library. He still occupied it in June 1815, during his last stay at Malmaison.

According to Laure Junot, who was a frequent visitor, "Our apartments consisted of a bedroom, a cabinet and a room for our maid... The furniture was very plain and the apartment of the daughter of the house, next to my own, differed from it only by a double door. Moreover, I believe she was only given this apartment after her marriage. I was surprised to see no parquetry on the bedroom floors... These rooms gave on to a long passage, to which one acceded by a step, leaving Mme Bonaparte's apartment and the small breakfast-room on the right. This passage was very narrow, tiled like the rest, and over-looking the courtyard." A few of the original tiles can still be seen at the bottom of a wood chest. There were then eight apartments on the first floor and ten on the second.

Concerning the gardens, Fontaine's ideas were classical and Josephine's romantic. In the end, it was she who got her way. By April 1800, the park, now extended as far as the St-Germain road, was enclosed. October 4th, "we are making place for various sports, to amuse the young aides-de-camp and all the young people comprising the family and court of the First Consul." In December, "we are enlarging the stables and the outhouses. We are making plans... for adding new ones". March 21st 1801, "the First Consul has ordered additions to the buildings used by his staff. The sentry's outpost and the gate will be removed to the stable near the road. We shall add to the little mill, a pavilion and a roundabout for the visitors' servants and coaches and get the outhouses ready as soon as possible to lodge a great many people."

12
P.-J. Redouté. Study of roses. Water-colour (gift Le Fuel).

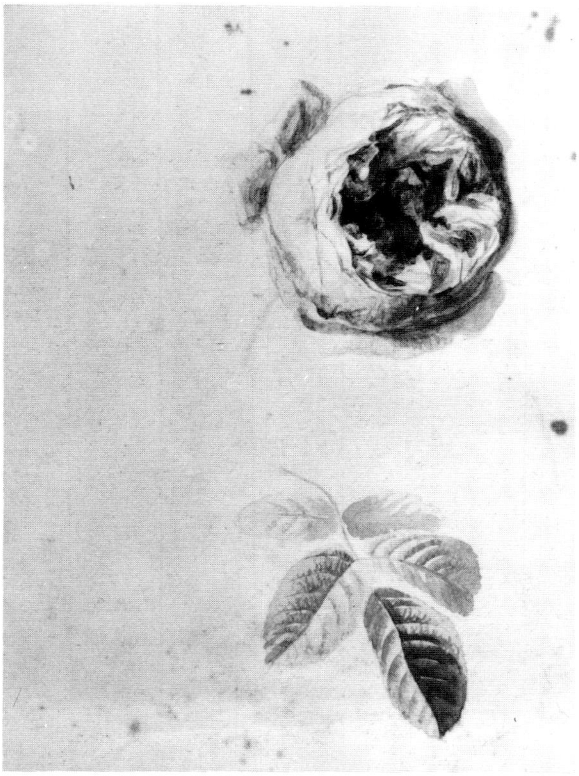

In 1801, after an attempt made on Bonaparte's life in the rue Nicaise, it became necessary to protect him by increasing his bodyguard. Fontaine states on December 16th: "From Menus-Plaisirs we took away the remains of some portable huts, and we made other small wooden huts in which we set up sentry-posts at the most important spots at Malmaison: one on the main road near the La Jonchère path, another one on top of the grey slope, a third one at the entry to Rueil and a fourth one by the walls of General Masséna's park (the latter had bought Richelieu's former château, nearer the village). The First Consul let us have our way, but he did not approve of these precautions; he has just ordered the suppression of these sentry-boxes, which are uninhabitable in cold weather and the completion of the building destined for a cavalry picket at the entry to the park on the Rueil side. This charming house, a veritable "Guides' Pavilion" still exists, as does a sentry-box rebuilt in durable materials, near by it.

"I know for certain," states the secretary Bourrienne, "that there have been several attempts to kidnap the First Consul... At first he sometimes visited the surroundings, but reports from the police made him more cautious and he began to fear that Royalist supporters might be in waiting to kidnap him."

On May 12th 1802, however, "The First Consul has bought the Butard Pavilion, between Marly and Versailles, and we have been ordered to arrange and set in order this little house, which will be used as a hunting-lodge." Laure Junot, the future duchesse d'Abrantès, tells how Napoleon forced Josephine in her carriage, to cross an awkward ford on its way, without taking any heed of her tears of fright. On April 4th 1801, Bonaparte had already bought the nearby pavilion of La Jonchère as a present for his step-son, Eugène de Beauharnais. Bourrienne had preferred to buy a cottage furnished by Bonaparte at Rueil, but " the First Consul often sent someone to wake me at night when courriers arrived."

Josephine was already taking a great interest in the park. Jealous Fontaine wrote on February 4th 1801, "Madame Bonaparte has engaged an English gardener who, like all artists of his kind, considers the planting we are engaged on to be all wrong." Howatson's reign lasted for five years. After having recommended Morel's work on gardens, the architect was annoyed when its author arrived in person next September "He was a little old man of seventy, robust in body and fairly clear in mind; everything we had done seemed to him insupportable... We had planned a botanical garden, with hot-houses, a menagery, aviaries, fish-pools and in the centre a small pavilion, containing a museum. This plan had been warmly received. One of the hothouses was already built; but the patriarch of "à l'anglaise" gardens found fault with everything. The hothouse was demolished."

October 2nd, "General Duroc informs us that the First Consul has appointed M. Lelieur de Ville-sur-Arce superintendant of the gardens." This was an old comrade-in-arms of Bonaparte's, whom he had charged with making a few economies. In vain. This costly fantasy was becoming a scientific passion. Méneval, Bourrienne's successor, notes: "The renewed peace with England allowed Josephine to enter into relations with various botanists and some of the chief horticulturists of London. From them... she received plants to enrich her collections. on these occasions she gave me letters in English to translate for her into French."

She frequently inspected the hothouses, which were already remarkable. One day she took the English minister Fox, on whom Napoleon counted a great deal, and his retinue. The statesman was delighted: "...Here are hydrangeas named in French "hortensias" after my daughter, alpine soldanella, Parma violets, lilies from the Nile, Damiette roses; these conquests from Italy and Egypt will make no enemies for Bonaparte. But here is my own conquest, she added, showing us a fine jasmine from Martinique; I sowed and cultivated the seed and it reminds me of my country, my childhood and the finery I wore when I was a girl. And when she spoke thus, her Creole voice truly seemed like a music full of expression and tenderness."

13
The small theatre at Malmaison. Pen and water-colour by the architect Fontaine (private collection).

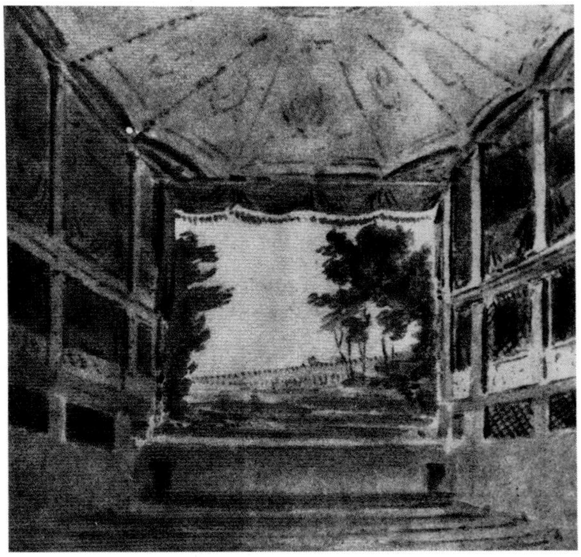

She chose specialists to advise her: Soulange-Bodin, nephew of her friend and adviser Calmelet, Ventenat, a member of the Institute, who dedicated to her his *The Garden of Malmaison,* of which the first volume, illustrated by the famous Redouté, appeared in 1803, then Brisseau de Mirbel who supervised the rare plants and made exchanges with various botanical gardens or private persons. In this way, nearly two hundred new species, not counting the foreign roses, were introduced into France.

Bonaparte and the young people preferred the theatre. Isabey recalls how they began with charades before attacking serious plays: The Barber of Seville, Distrust and Malice, Crispin rival of his master, False Confidences, The Miser, The Litigants... "Our producers were Mlle Hortense and her brother Eugène de Beauharnais, our masters: Talma, Michot, Fleury and Mlle Mars."

Fontaine, always exact, notes on March 22nd, 1802: "We have made a sort of portable theatre which can be set up in the gallery of Malmaison, near the drawing-room. Then we found a way of making a small hall out of a diagonal portion of one of the largest rooms at the 2nd floor in the North Pavilion (this was later to become the Empress' wardrobe); but though this arrangement gave us more room than the first, it was less suitable for our requirements. One had to go up two floors, leaving the drawing-rooms and the guests for a narrow room without space or elegance. Finally the First Consul gave in... and ordered us to build, as economically as possible, a small hall, entirely isolated, in the direction of the farm. He gave us a month to carry out this work... A plan and an estimate were drawn up yesterday and the whole thing has been handed over to M. Bourrienne who, with Mlle Hortense,.. is one of our most enthusiastic actors. Here is the letter we have sent him on this subject:

"...We find it would be possible to make in thirty days and for the sum of 30 000 F,... a theatre-hall... built of planks and practically movable if this is desired. The form is circular, with sections to break it up, the whole covered with slate tiles. There will be a pit, a row of boxes, a gallery, an orchestra, two small foyers and a theatre without any machinery... The ceiling, like the inner walls, will be covered with painted canvas. The low floor will be raised above the ground-level to avoid damp and disposed in such a way that it can be used as a ball-room if necessary. It will hold at least two hundred people..."

By April 20th, "the little theatre... is ready... as we promised". May 12th. "the theatre of Malmaison has been used for the first time. The Italians acted the *Serva Padrona*. The place seemed very pleasant and if the play had been more to the taste of the audience, they would have enjoyed themselves very much."

As a matter of fact, regular visitors to Malmaison preferred to do the acting themselves. Though neither he nor Josephine ever went on the stage, "Napoleon went regularly to the theatre... and really enjoyed himself", according to Méneval. "I cannot refrain from saying how much we enjoyed seeing our employers dressed up in this way", declared the valet Constant. According to Bourrienne: "Hortense acted marvellously, Caroline rather badly, Eugène very well, Lauriston (the aide-de-camp) was a bit heavy, Didelot (the Prefect of the palace) fair, and I dare to claim... that I was not the worst of the company. Anyway, if we were not good, it was not for lack of good lessons and advice: Talma and Michot came to rehearse us, sometimes all together and sometimes individually... Bonaparte gave each of us a collection of plays, very well bound... he had had some rich, elegant costumes made for us... sometimes he even paid us compliments. Though all this amused me as much as it did the others, I was sometimes obliged to point out to him that my occupations did not leave me much time to learn my parts: then he put on his affectionate manner and said: "Come on, don't tell me that, you have such a good memory! You know it amuses me:... get up earlier. — I sleep a lot, don't I?" — "Come on, Bourrienne, do it for me. You always manage to make me laugh. Don't deprive me of this pleasure. I don't get much, you know..."

"There were always a great many people at Malmaison when there was a performance. After the spectacle, there was a crowd in the ground-floor apartments. There were all kinds of refreshments... These delightful evenings generally ended about midnight and the guests took the road back to Paris."

Laure Junot confirms Bourrienne's account; performances were on Wednesdays and "the First Consul... nearly always invited forty people to dinner and a hundred and fifty to spend the evening — that is to say, to listen to us, judge us and mock us pitilessly. Our audience was composed of consuls, ministers, the diplomatic corps, the State counsellors, senators, their wives and the whole military establishment... This was impressive enough, but the worst bogy was the Frist Consul himself. He would be there in his box, close beside us, and he followed us with his eyes and at the same time with a more or less mocking smile, which terrified us all."

On July 1st, 1802, Fontaine's mission was accomplished: "We have just received from General Duroc, the order to hand over the direction of the work at Malmaison to M. Lepère, architect, returned from Egypt." The latter was not kept so busy, since Bonaparte had decided Malmaison was not sufficiently grand and was restoring the château at Saint-Cloud. By May 1801, over 600 000 F had already been spent on Malmaison, which was now a model of the consular style, antique certainly, but full of elegant variety, the only domain where one can really imagine the Bonaparte couple in their daily life.

Malmaison is still impregnated with memories of the brilliant life of this period and many accounts have come down to us: "Nowhere, except perhaps on the battlefield, have I seen Bonaparte happier than in his gardens at Malmaison... There, Bonaparte sometimes neglected his work in order to take walks and supervise personally the improvements which he had ordered... after dinner, he amused himself by calculating the income from the grounds. He forgot neither the upkeep of the park nor the vegetables in the kitchen garden. His accounts showed an income of 8 000 F. "That's not bad," he said to me," "but one needs a yearly income of 30 000 to live there" (Bourrienne). The sound of the church bell at Rueil moved him because it reminded him of his childhood. "The people need a religion", he said to Thibaudet as he heard it ring. For Malmaison, he preferred to choose former masters or servants of his youth, such as father Dupuy, formerly "headmaster" of the College at Brienne, who was now the librarian, or Hauté, ex-porter of the college, promoted to watch over the inner gate of the château.

Here he found familiar faces, received his family and chosen guests. Josephine rose late and took a long time over her toilet before lunching with her daughter and some women-guests at about eleven o'clock in a small dining-room near her apartment. Bonaparte had been at work since at least seven o'clock with Bourrienne in his study, where he lunched rapidly and alone off a pedestal table at about ten o'clock. Family dinner was eaten in the dining-room at about six in the afternoon. "There was only one table. The First Consul sat at one side, with Mme Louis Bonaparte next to him, while Mme Bonaparte sat opposite. The First Consul's aides-de-camp and his establishment had access to his table; there was generally one of the Consuls, a minister, one or two ladies among the guests, rarely a stranger." (Méneval). "When it was fine, the First Consul ordered his meal to be served in the park. The table was set up to the left of the lawn in front of the château, just before the straight drive... We did not stay long at table; theFirst Consul found the dinner long if it lasted half-an-hour" (duchesse d'Abrantès). Scientists like Monge and Volney, and actors were invited in turn. Mme Hulot, General Moreau's mother-in-law, once forced her way in, to Bonaparte's obvious displeasure. He often tried to disconcert his guests by putting abrupt questions, and he appreciated rapid, witty replies. He himself liked making jokes, some of them clumsy ones.

14
The Empress Josephine in her coronation robe, painting after François Gérard
(gift of Mrs. Helen Fahnestock-Hubbard, 1938).

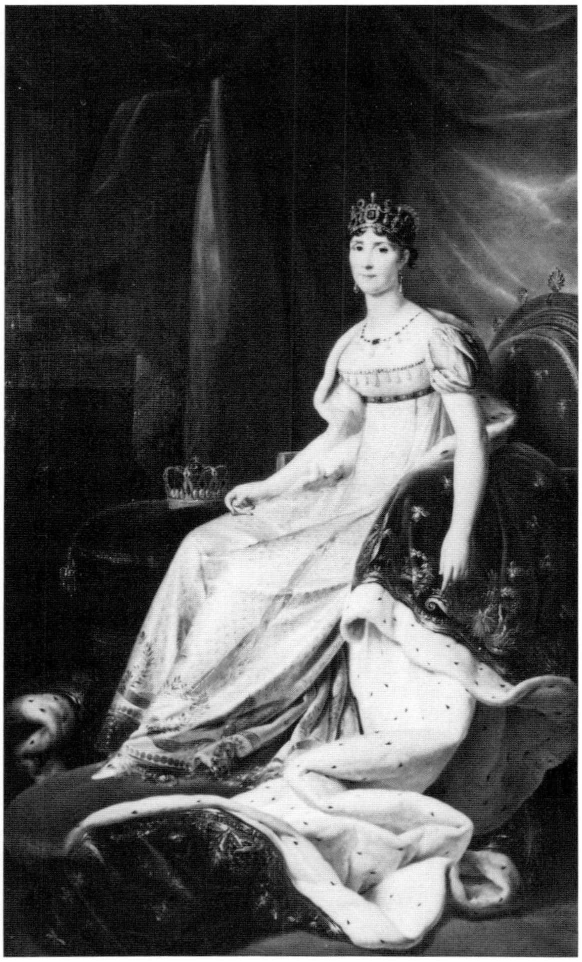

The Consul took part in open-air sports: "When he was up early and the weather was fine... he played at prisoners' base with us. There he cheated as he did at cards; he tripped us up, came up on us without crying: *barre*!... On such occasions, Napoleon took off his coat and ran like a hare, or rather, like the gazelle he fed with all the tobacco from his pouch, encouraging it to run at us, and the horrid animal tore our dresses and often our legs" (duchesse d'Abrantès).

On fine evenings, he walked arm-in-arm with Josephine, leaving Hortense and her friends in the drawing-room with the aides-de-camp, who intimidated them. At Malmaison, love-affairs were started, engagements arranged. Hortense preferred Duroc, who was deeply in love with her, but was forced to marry Louis, the Consul's sickly younger brother. The couple spent a rather gloomy honeymoon at Malmaison in January 1802. The evenings were spent in playing chess, reversi, vingt et un or backgammon, or Josephine laid out the cards for a patience.

Hortense relates in her memoirs that Napoleon "sent for a new book and wanted me to read aloud. I was so embarrassed at doing this in front of him and his staff that I could not see a word. Then he said to me: "Doesn't Mme Campan teach you to read?" and this made me even more embarrassed. One day he brought *Atala*, which had just been published... It was as if I was spelling it out and I looked so miserable that the Consul told me to stop after a few pages..."

Luckily, there was dancing, at which Hortense excelled. Bonaparte sometimes took part in the Sunday evening balls. "His favourite dance was the Monaco: at least, he said, one got some good exercise." (Isabey) Hortense led wild farandoles through the whole house. The Press reported a more important ball given on August 15th 1802 in honour of the Consul's birthday. Though Hortense was pregnant, she was forced to dance at the request of her stepfather. This was in order to give the lie to the English Press, which had published the news of her confinement. "Bonaparte had been shocked and indignant at this premature announcement which he realised was intended to accredit certain libellous rumours of his own liaison with Hortense" (Bourrienne).

Malmaison was also a political centre, where important events sometimes took place and where the First Consul liked to reflect and take decisions.

There, Josephine anxiously awaited news of the "reserve Army". Fontaine notes that on July 2nd 1800 "we had news of the victory of Marengo. Mme Bonaparte gave a supper under the trees in the small garden... We put up tents, lent by Lecomte (the architect of the Tuileries), to roof the tables." According to the tradition, it was then that Josephine planted a cedar... the "Marengo cedar", grown today into a majestic tree.

On October 23rd a fête was held in honour of General Moreau, Bonaparte's rival who still had to be handled with tact.

Although she states that "there was never any question of politics in the drawing-room", Hortense had to admit that on June 30th, 1801, "My mother presented me a lady who had arrived from England and came only once to Malmaison. This was the duchesse de Guiche. She did not see the Consul." This was the daughter of Mme de Polignac, the friend of Marie-Antoinette, come to find out if there was any hope of a restoration. When the Vendée was pacified, "the leaders who came to Malmaison were well received by the Consul; he seemed to have special consideration for them." On October 1st, Bonaparte, overjoyed, told the ladies, before informing Talleyrand, of the ratification of the preliminaries for peace with England. After the attempt on his life, sharp words were exchanged in the drawing-room between Napoleon and Fouché: "Mme Bonaparte, who was very fond of Fouché... came up behind Bonaparte and slipped her hand through his arm, the FirstConsul gently disengaged his arm from the pressure of his wife's and said, not crossly but in a peremptory way: "Josephine, please don't interfere when I am having a serious discussion." (Laure d'Abrantès). The Minister of the Police won the day however: "On Saturday, January 31st, 1801, about two hours after our arrival at Malmaison, we saw Fouché arrive bringing authentic proofs that he had been right in his previsions... Then Bonaparte saw clear as daylight that the attempt on his life of 3 nivôse had been plotted by royalist supporters" (Bourrienne).

Luckily there were other, less distressing scenes at Malmaison and sometimes ridiculous. After ceding Tuscany to the In-

15
Mahogany pedestal-table, original furniture of Malmaison (?)
(gift Marquet).

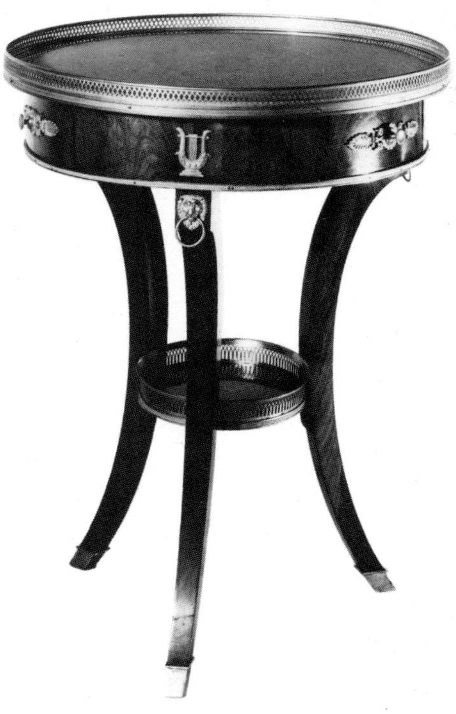

fante of Parma, the King of Spain's son-in-law, in exchange for the reunion of Parma with France, Bonaparte decided to receive the "King of Etruria" at Malmaison on his way to Florence. "This was the first throne presented by Bonaparte and the first Bourbon to reappear in France since the Revolution", Hortense rightly remarks. The young couple travelled under the names of the Count and Countess de Livourne. On May 26th, 1801, the King was received by the Consul "who had a long talk with him in the gallery of Malmaison. No preparations were made for this new sovereign". However, "before he was due to arrive... we put in place two of the four paintings executed for the decoration of the drawing-room: one of them showed the First Consul lying down, exhausted, during the crossing of the Alps, before the victory of Marengo, with the marching soldiers careful not to disturb his sleep; in the other, the First Consul stands on the summit of the Alps, showing his Army the rich plains of Lombardy. The First Consul came in as they were being hung. He looked at them angrily and ordered that they should be taken down at once. The green hangings they had replaced were quickly put back and the two paintings had disappeared by the time the King of Etruria arrived." (Fontaine). Bourrienne confirms the event in a livelier style: "The First Consul emerged for a moment from his study. He wanted to be sure the drawing-room was ready for the reception of the Prince. He returned almost immediately and said to me in a nervous, angry way: "Bourrienne, can you imagine their stupidity? They wanted the Prince to see a painting showing me pointing to Lombardy from the peak of the Alps and ordering its conquest. I soon had it taken down. It was completely unsuitable."

16
Books preserved at Malmaison, from the Emperor's library and the original Malmaison library.

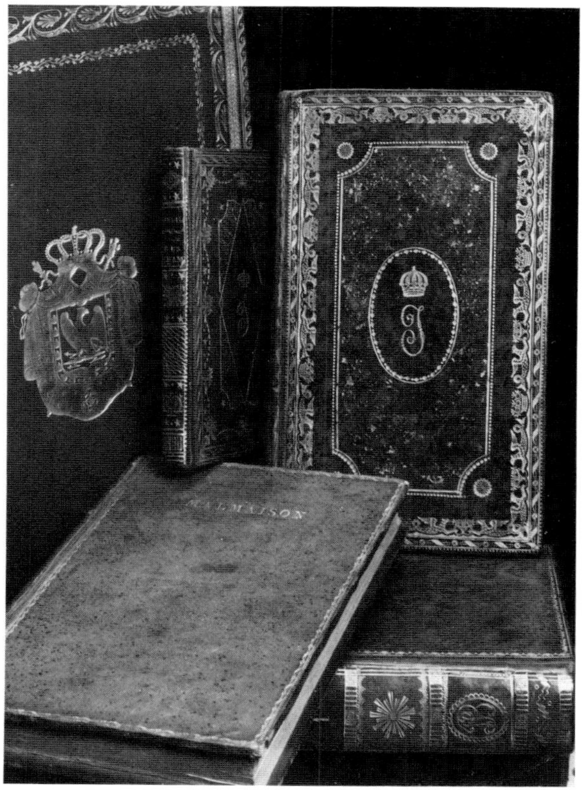

According to Hortense: "the King was tall and well made. His face, with its sagging cheeks and thick lips, was expressionless. He was subject to fits of epilepsy. They often came to Malmaison but the Consul took no notice of them after the first day. He was too busy with other things. My mother was ill, so I was alone and had to receive them. They were easily amused, delighted by everything — the walks, music, games of prisoners' base and other parlour games. When the Consul wanted to talk business with the King and explain how he should reign, he found him so inattentive that he scolded me laughingly for making him forget his kingdom." Bourrienne confirms these recollections: "The King and Queen dined several times at Malmaison. Once, the King fainted; he said this was caused by indigestion but his servants whispered that he had had a fit... The comte de Livourne... was really childish. The First Consul heard indirectly of all the stupidities committed by this prince when he came to Malmaison: he did not see them himself, since he was constantly at work. I heard him groan over the Prince's nullity". If we are to believe Fontaine, he even gave up at the last minute the idea of holding a reception for him (May 28th, 1801): "There was to be a fête, a great feast at Malmaison and we had ordered for it an octagonal tent, fifty feet wide. This tent was to be set up like a sort of great umbrella outside the hall, at the end of the small bridge and near the lawn. The main part of the framework was ready but when the First Consul was asked for some more money to finish it, he countermanded the whole thing and we had to ask the carpenter

Bouillier, who had constructed it, to keep it until it could be used." There were merely fêtes organized by Berthier and Talleyrand in honour of the new king.

Certain treaties were signed in this country residence, such as the "Act of Malmaison", the draft of a federal constitution for Switzerland, on April 29th, 1801; on May 2nd a conference was held there with Mgr Spina, a roman representative, Talleyrand and Bernier, on the subject of the Concordat; Cardinal Consalvi, Secretary of State, came to dinner on July 2nd; on October 2nd the Treaty of Saint Ildefonse was ratified by which Spain returned Louisiana, soon to be ceded to the United States.

So many Councils were held at Malmaison during these crucial years! Roederer recalls some of them. On April 10th, 1802, "the Secretary of State has the honour of informing the citizen Roederer that the First Consul desires him to come to Malmaison today, between twelve and one o'clock, for a Council Extraordinary."

"We discussed the question: "Should the First Consul kiss the paten? "— The First Consul said sharply to Portalis: "Don't make me do such a ridiculous thing." Next day: "Council Extraordinary at Malmaison: the three Consuls, the Minister of the Interior, Régnier, Portalis and myself. We planned the Easter ceremony at Notre-Dame. The First Consul wanted the government to go only to the Te Deum, while Portalis and Régnier insisted for the Mass. The First Consul asked that he should be spared kissing the paten and anything that would make him look ridiculous."

These details become significant when one remembers that this ceremony, which the government had to attend after the promulgation of the Concordat, was strongly opposed in political and military circles. The session ended with a discussion of an extensive amnisty for emigrés.

Early in May, Roederer received from Malmaison the minutes of the draft bill for the creation of the Legion of Honour, which he was to propose to the State Council then to the Legislative Assembly. In July, Bonaparte awaited at Malmaison the result of the vote on the life tenure of the Consulate. On the 22nd, Roederer went "with the Consul Lebrun to Malmaison. The Consul Cambaracérès had brought Portalis and Muraire. There was a privy Council, composed of the three Consuls ans we four State Councillors."

"The object of this Council was to communicate to us the First Consul's plan for modifying the political organisation of France"...

After a discussion lasting two hours and a half, the First Consul ordered us to meet next day; to draw up the notes... to return to Malmaison at 8 o'clock." And the Councils continued at the same rythm till August 14th, in Paris or at the Malmaison! The reform of the constitution was then promulgated.

It was at this period that Bonaparte spent the longest time in

17
Mahogany and bronze paper-holder with the arms of Empress Josephine, by Biennais
(gift of Empress Eugénie).

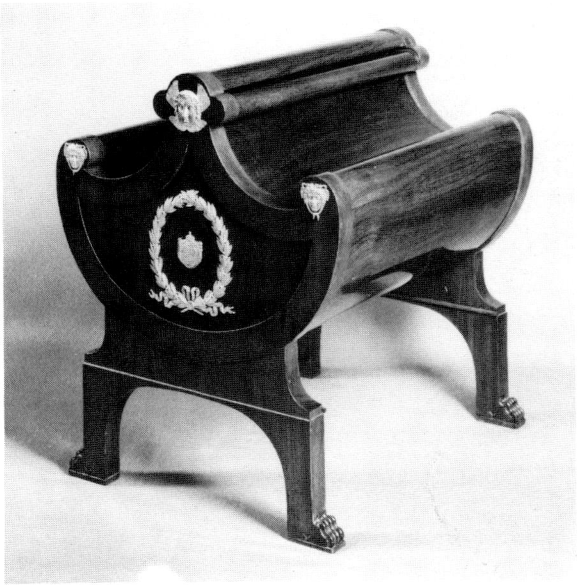

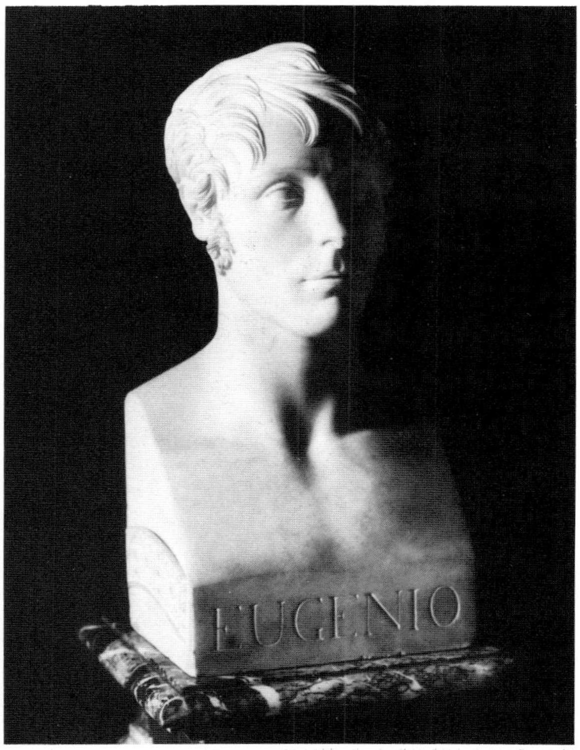

18 Giovanni-Battista Comolli (1775-1830). Prince Eugène, Viceroy of Italy. Marble bust, signed and dated 1809. Former collection of Malmaison.

19 François-Joseph Bosio (1768-1845). Queen Hortense, marble bust, 1810. Former collection of Malmaison (?) (gift Mariano de Unzue, 1929).

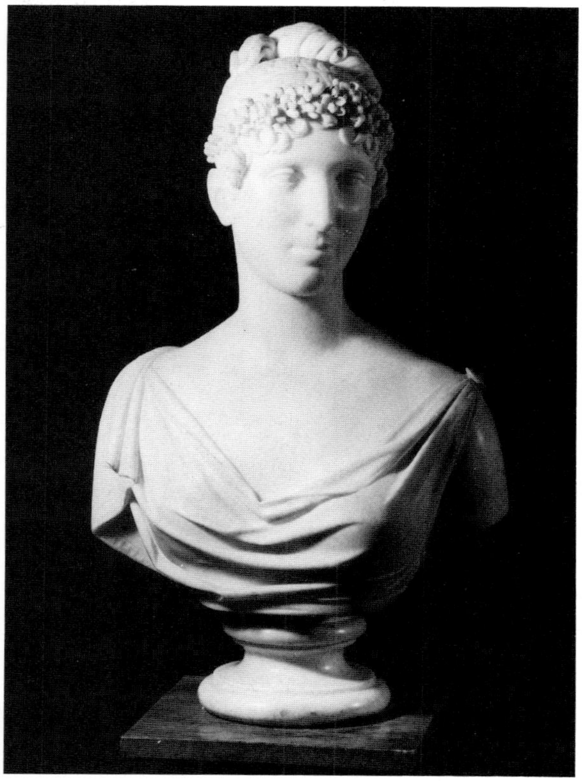

his domain, before he went to live at Saint-Cloud, which was larger and more practical and was ready for him by the end of September. Though Malmaison was not neglected, it became the Marly or the Trianon of this new Versailles. According to Bourrienne, "one of his first cares was to repare the short-cut leading from Saint-Cloud to Malmaison; Bonaparte could do it in quarter of an hour."

Malmaison had also the sad privilege of seeing more dramatic events during the Consulate when the plot woven by Cadoudal, Pichegru and Moreau was discovered, and when the duc d'Enghien was arrested and put to death. Between March 12th and 23rd, Bonaparte was at Malmaison where he held council every day. "Georges" was arrested on the evening of the 9th and on the 10th came the order to seize the duc d'Enghien. The Prince was taken to Vincennes and shot on the night of the 21st-22nd. Mme de Rémusat, Hortense, Méneval — all more reliable witnesses than Bourrienne, who had fallen out of favour — recall the atmosphere of anguish that reigned at Malmaison, Josephine's vain pleadings for the prisoner, Napoleon's oppressive silence or false gaiety, his despondancy when the fatal news was brought on the 22nd at eight in the morning. The Consul has accepted his responsabilities. Yet we cannot help thinking that if he had not been relatively far from the place where the tragedy was being enacted, he would have been informed hour by hour of the progress of the trial, and might have granted a reprieve, as he has so often done. This execution brought the final rupture with the Bourbons, the end of all Josephine's dreams of some kind of restoration of the "Ancien Régime"; it foreshadowed the Empire and the gradual abandon of Malmaison in favour of the former châteaux of the monarchy.

Malmaison under the Empire

Malmaison was not abandoned during the first years of the Empire though Napoleon stayed there less and less: four days in July 1804, ten in February 1805, ten in March, two in September, nine in March-April 1806. Next year, he arrived on March 19th for St. Joseph's day, celebrated by a theatrical performance, fireworks and a ball in the New Gallery. He left on the 22nd. A final fête was held on December 1st in honour of the sovereigns present in Paris. Josephine, however, managed to spend eight months there, often alone, during the Emperor's campaigns. She enlarged the domain with all the available grounds around it, bought the Saint-Cucufa wood and the former château of Buzenval, had a splendid hothouse erected in 1805 by Jean-Thomas Thibaut and Barthélemy Vignon, with a gallery, a salon decorated soon after with a marble *Cupid* by Bosio, a dairy, a vast sheep-fold holding 500 Spanish merinos. She amused herself by transforming the park, stocking it with animals at liberty, and multiplying the "fabriques", with the help of the architect Berthault and the erudite Alexandre Lenoir (Naumachia, or Neptune's Pool, Temple of Love decorated with a statue by Tassaert, a grotto for a "Grey friar" in fact a terra-cotta statue of *St Francis receiving the stigmata*, by Germain Pilon, a masterpiece; and a "tumular monument" decorated with a relief of *Sorrow* from the tomb of the Princess de Conti).

Nothing could discourage her from creating a real "experimental garden" open to specialists. A note published in May 1805 in the *Magasin encyclopédique* confirms that "H.M. the Empress, desiring that her important collection of plants and animals should serve the advancement of science, has ordered that Malmaison should be open to members of the Institute and to the administrators of the Natural History Museum." Captain Baudin, returning from his expedition to the Autral regions, sent her a gnu, a zebra, black swans, which she thus introduced for the first time into Europe, and emus from King Island in the Bass detroit, a species which has now disappeared, which she ceded to the Museum. The King of Saxony presented her with a couple of kangaroos in 1806. General Thiébault, governor of Fulda in 1807, discovered a chamois in the grounds of the château and sent it to Malmaison. The Prefect Thibaudeau begged the Empress's patronage for the botanical garden he was creating in Marseilles and exchanged plants with the hothouses at Malmaison. Josephine wrote him a personal letter, as she did to her brother-in-law, the Marquis de Beauharnais, ambassador to Spain, and to Count Daru, Superintendant General. In 1807, the latter sent her from Berlin notes on the flora of Pomerania. She wrote in her turn: "I hear there are some very rare plants in the gardens of the Elector of Hesse and in those of Hanover. I think these collections would be worth your attention." She repeated her demands when he was in Vienna in September 1809.

In 1805, the English gardener Howatson was succeeded by Félix Delahaye, formerly chief gardener in d'Entrecasteaux's expedition, while between 1803 and 1806, Brisseau de Mirbel was "superintendant of the gardens" and Ventenat published descriptions of rare species. The latter died in 1808 and was replaced by Aimé Goujaud, known as Bonpland, a former companion of Alexandre de Humboldt, who combined the superintendance of the gardens with the study of their plants and left Malmaison only to undertake well-defined missions in Berlin and Vienna. Pierre-Joseph Redouté was appointed in 1805 "flower-painter to the Empress" with an annual salary of 18,000 F. He industriously produced wonderful hand-painted prints to illustrate the delivery of *Liliaceous plants, Roses, Rare Plants cultivated at Malmaison and at Navarre*. French nursery-men like André Du Pont, Guerrapain, Vilmorin, and foreigners, especially the Englishmen Lee and Kennedy, continued to sent specimens to Malmaison in spite of the war and the blockade.

The Empress's passion for natural science was such that she accepted collections of naturalised animals, mounted birds, stuffed mammiferians, all chosen with the help of Louis Dufresne and part of which she gave to the Museum in 1808. There were also collections of shells and minerals made by the naturalist Antoine-Marie Héron de Villefosse, arranged in elegant boxes in the form of bound books, or acquired in 1807 from Besson, a former inspector of mines. Extremely rare ethnographical objects, especially Polynesian ones, were brought to her from the Baudin expedition.

Josephine should not, however, be considered a blue stocking. She was nearly as interested in the arts, ancient or modern, as in flowers, jewels and finery. On the sensible advice

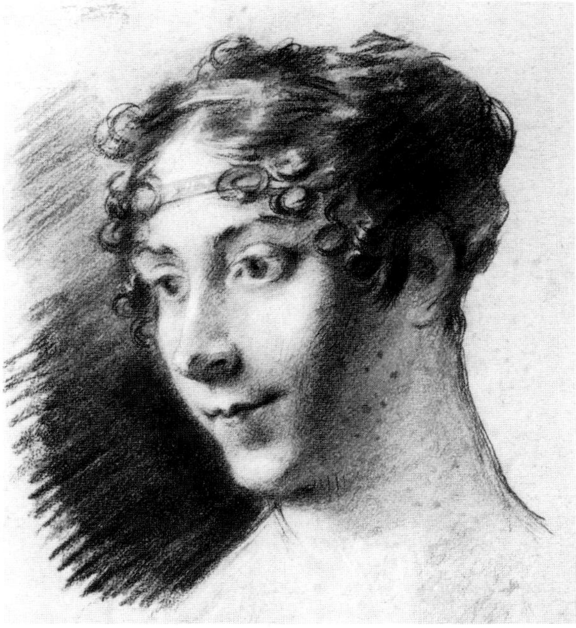

20
Pierre-Paul Prud'hon (after). Empress Josephine, charcoal drawing, study for the large portrait of 1805 (Bequest of Mlle Hochon, 1953).

21
Antonio Canora (1757-1822) (after). Napoleon, First Consul, large bust, marble.

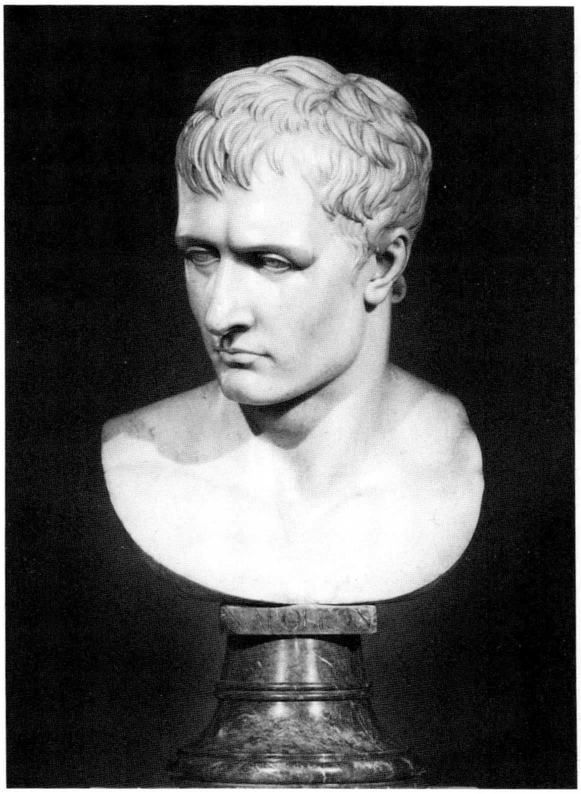

of Denon, Alexandre Lenoir, and the merchant-restorer Constantin, she bought at the Salons, launched young painters, managed to get most of the artistic treasures from the Emperor's conquests entrusted to her, especially the Elector of Hesse's magnificent collection of paintings in 1806, till finally the architect Berthault had to raise the "Great Gallery" with its top-lighting, to house them. This has now been demolished but it was then a veritable museum, prolonging the "Small Gallery" to the East, with its Rembrandts and Rubens, Gerard Dou and Metsu, Potter and Wouverman, Van Dyck and Ruysdael, Poussin and Claude Lorrain, Bellini and Corregio, Raphael and da Vinci, Titien and Veronese, the Carraches and a certain number of Spaniards, not to mention the marbles, bronzes, mosaics, paintings, antique vases and "curiosities" from Egypt and elsewhere. This excessive proliferation in such a modest domain was certainly due to Napoleon's long absences.

Malmaison after the divorce

22
Bronze Victory by Chaudet, 1810. It was formerly held in the left hand of the imperial statue on the summit of the Column of the Great Army, place Vendôme
(gift of Mrs. Francis Doucha Oakes, 1966).

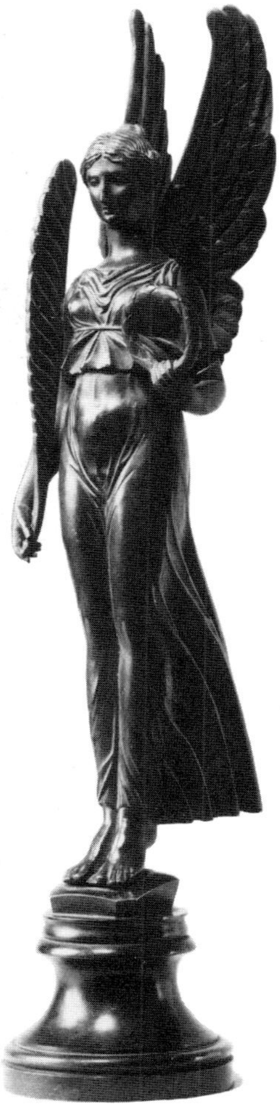

Josephine had been unable to give the Emperor the heir he so ardently desired. There had been threats of divorce for a long time and it finally came about on December 15th 1809. The repudiated Empress had this been right to embellish Malmaison, since full ownership was attributed to her, together with that of the château of Navarre, near Evreux.

Queen Hortense evokes the rupture in her memoirs: "Early next morning, I went to my mother. Her drawing-room was full of ladies of the Palace, weeping over her departure... I drove my mother away in the carriage while the Emperor was in Council. He had said goodbye to her earlier... We were sad and silent all the way to Malmaison. Her heart was heavy as she entered this place she loved so much. "If he is happy," she said, "I shall not regret it", and her eyes filled constantly with tears."

"The day after she left the Tuileries, the Emperor paid her a visit... He took her hand in a friendly way and they walked for a long time near the château, talking together. Every day, he sent a page with a letter... But the days passed. The letters became less frequent and she was constantly waiting for them. She had a small cabinet from which she could see the main road. Whenever she heard there was to be a hunt in the forest of Saint-Germain, she stayed at the window till she had seen the Emperor's carriage pass and pass back. Little by little, she seemed to resign herself... Moreover, Malmaison was always crowded with people, from the humblest merchant to ministers and marshals, come to lay their respects and homage at her feet". The duchesse d'Abrantès came to Malmaison with Madame Duchâtel the day after the divorce: "The Empress received anyone who wanted to pay his respects. The drawing-room, billiard-room and gallery were full of people... As for the Empress, she had never looked better: she sat on the right of the fireplace, under the fine painting by Girodet, very simply dressed, with a wide green hood on her head which could serve when necessary to hide her tears... She raised her eyes on each person who entered and smiled at him... but if this person was one of her old friends, tears flowed at once down her cheeks, effortlessly, without any of the contractions which make a woman's face so ugly when she cries... All the crowned heads, majesties, highnesses, who were in Paris during that winter 1810, came to Malmaison to bow to the Empress. These visits were painful, yet they made her happy because they proved that the Emperor desired she should still be honoured as his *chosen wife*; at least, that was my impression one morning when I was at Malmaison."

The Prefect Thibaudeau was less lenient. He reports a conversation concerning the choice of the new Empress. Josephine openly deplored the vanity of the Emperor in wishing to marry a foreign princess, a Russian or an Austrian, rather than a Frenchwoman. Other contemporaries portray her as favourable to the Austrian marriage, which took place on April 2nd.

Napoleon continued to watch over her tenderly. He allowed her an important "establishment": a lady-in-waiting, the Countess d'Arberg, nine ladies attached to the palace, a chaplain, chamberlains, including the charming painter Turpin de Crissé, equerries, a knight of honour, a reader, a doctor, a head secretary, a superintendant-general (Comte de Montlivault succeeded Pierlot in June 1811) four ladies of the bedchamber, at least thirty-six persons, without counting the servants. He made her a present of the neighbouring domain of Bois-Préau, which she had long wanted, and there she lodged part of her Court and the surplus of her collections.

A new existence began now — one which was both futile and very busy. Memories of the past were carefully cultivated. The Emperor's apartment was preserved untouched, if we are to believe the Countess de Kielmansegge: the Empress... "took me into the library which had once been the Emperor's bedchamber and in which every object was still exactly in the place he had left it. Her emotion grew as she showed me one thing after another. The last object she pointed out was the worn armchair of black morocco leather which he had slashed all over with his penknife. Then unable to contain herself any longer, she burst into tears". Comtesse Potocka visited Malmaison in the summer of 1810, after Josephine had left for Switzerland: "Napoleon's bedchamber... was still exactly as he had left it never to return! Josephine allowed noone to enter it. We had to insist and pay heavily before we could get someone to show it to us... Malmaison should become the property of the nation. Apart from the interest attached to the least details of the life of a great man, this room is in itself one of the most beautiful one could hope to see. The carved bed is of antique shape, simple and perfect; it is placed on a stage covered with an enormous tiger skin of the greatest beauty. In place of curtains, there is a large tent held up by trophies of weapons recalling a victory or symbolizing a conquest..."

"Josephine's apartment was remarkable only for its lack of taste and harmony. The furniture is of all colours and all styles; — it's a mass of baubles quite devoid of simple elegance or

23
Jean-Pierre-Antoine Tassaert (1727-1788). Cupid preparing to shoot an arrow. Marble statue, formerly in the Temple of Love.

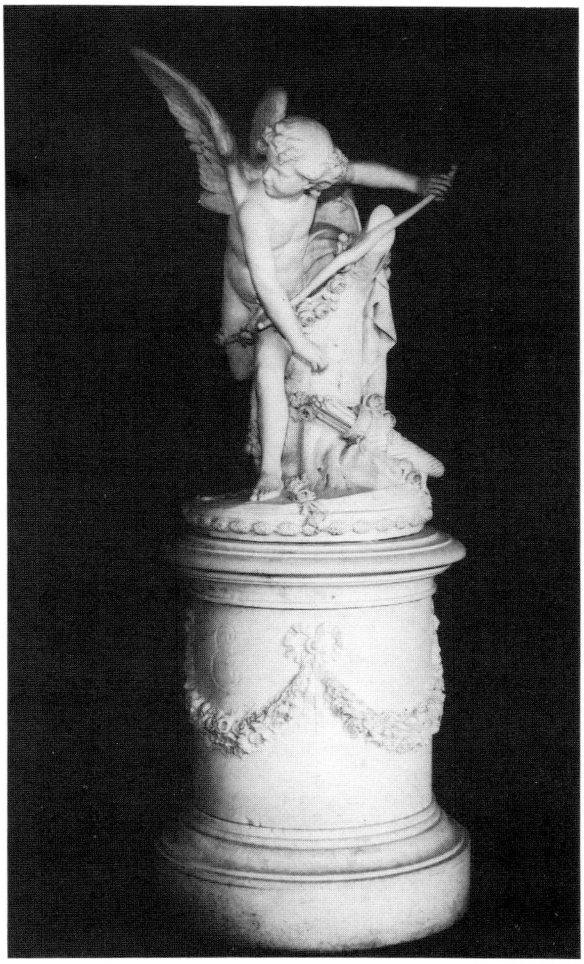

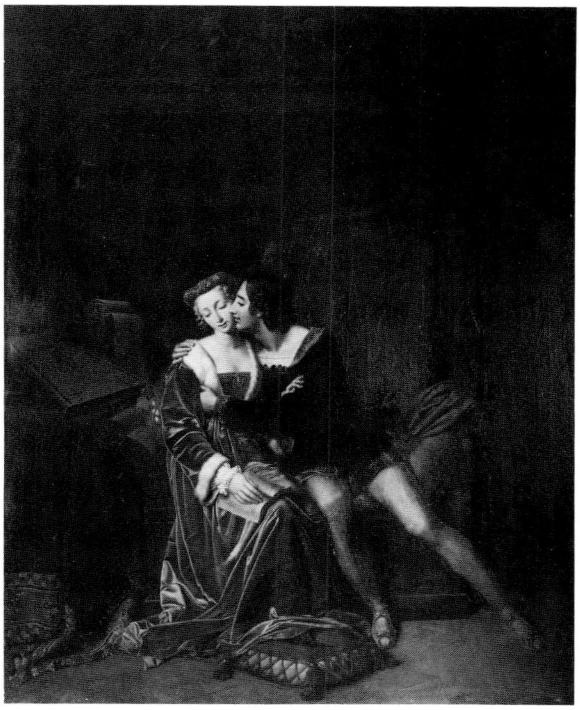

24
Marie-Philippe Coupin de la Couperie (1773-1851). The tragic love of Paolo Malatesta and Francesca da Rimini. This painting figured in the Empress's collections at Malmaison (Arenenberg, Switzerland, Napoleonmuseum).

25
Porcelaine plate from the Royal Manufactory of Berlin. From the Exotic Plants set presented to the Empress in 1807. Mesembryanthemum carinatum, Cape of Good Hope (gift of Dr Kölmann, 1973).

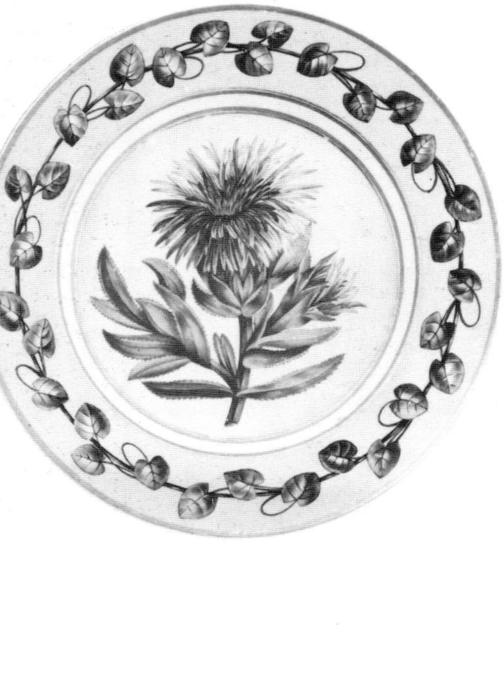

artistic, – no souvenirs, everything is recent. Fashion is all-powerful in Paris and here it reigns supreme."... This room was to be entirely altered in 1812.

"The picture gallery alone cannot be criticized. It is easy to see it was planned by an artist of taste and ability..."

"As for the architecture of the house, it is not only faulty but vulgar. The low main building looks squashed beneath the mansarded roof; the windows are small and narrow, the doors wretched, a few heavy decorations, in one word, meanness without simplicity, and pretentiousness without grandeur."

"The gardens, and specially the hothouses are admirable. There are so many rare plants from all parts of the world, that one might believe oneself to be in the tropics."

Georgette Ducrest, a member of Josephine's little Court, is more guarded than the young Polishwoman: "The Empress had kept a veritable cult for the Emperor and would not allow so much as a chair to be moved in the apartment he had occupied: and rather than live in it herself, she preferred to be very uncomfortably lodged on the first floor. Everything remained just as it was when the Emperor took leave of his study; a book of history on his writing table was marked at the page where he left off reading... a globe, on which he used to show his confidents the lands he planned to conquer, bore the marks of certain impatient movements... Josephine herself dusted what she called her relics and she seldom allowed anyone to enter this sanctuary."

"Napoleon's Roman bed had no curtains, there were weapons hanging on the walls of his bedchamber and a few pieces of clothing were still scattered on the furniture..."

"The ground-floor was truly magnificent, with a lot of mosaic tables from Florence and clocks of lapis or agate, beautifully worked bronzes and Sèvres porcelaines, offered by the Emperor. The furniture in the drawing-room was covered in tapestry, worked by the Empress, the background of white silk and the double J intertwined with fairy roses; when there were not many guests, this was protected by grey covers of gros-de-Naples. Josephine's apartment was extremely simple, with draperies of white muslin. It is true that the gold (sic for silver-gilt) toilet-set presented by the town, was worthy of its owner, nothing could have rivalled the richness of these objects; thus it stood apart from all the rest. Her Majesty had wanted several times to send it to the Vice-Reine, but Prince Eugène opposed this in my presence. It was a personal gift made to her at the time of her coronation. Napoleon sent it to her when they were divorced, together with a gold dinner-set and several other valuable things she had forgotten to take with her..."

The comte de Clary et Aldringen, grandson of the prince de Ligne, had been sent to Paris by the Emperor of Austria and has left a lively account of his visit to Malmaison on May 30th, 1810, in company with his cousin, Flore de Ligne. He was enthusiastic over the park, the hothouse and the drawing-room... "One can understand why that poor Empress Josephine adores Malmaison... Now all the kings and queens, the Grand-Duke of Wurtzbourg, all the Talleyrands, Mme Juste de Noailles, see her and cultivate her friendship; Mme de Metternich visits her there. All around Malmaison, the roads are full of six-horse carriages coming and going, of courriers and riders. In spite of all that, the Empress Josephine does not exactly entertain and no foreigners are introduced to her..."

"The Empress Josephine is a good woman: everyone regrets her and noone speaks ill of her: she has never harmed anyone. She is very frivolous and incapable of amusing herself with anything except botany; she needs to be constantly surrounded by people so that she finds herself bored and unhappy now."

"Even now that the Empress Josephine entertains in reality very little, one sees Leroy's gig every morning and even twice a day, coming to Malmaison for him to do her hair."

"A whole crowd of pages, chamberlains I believe, braided footmen, Basques (for the Empress has several Basques with very pretty costumes and who seem very agile), looked us up and down with surprise and finally led us to the entresol inhabited by Mme d'Audenarde (lady-in waiting). She received us with open arms... then asked us if we would like to see the gallery. We were dying to, so she went to the Empress and said:

"Will your Majesty be going to the gallery this morning?"
"Yes, the workmen are there, hanging some pictures."
"In that case I dare not put my request to your Majesty."
"What is the matter?"
"The princesse de Ligne and the comte de Clary have come to see me and I should have liked to show them the gallery."
"Well, take them, and I shall be there myself."

"Mme d'Audenarde then came to fetch us and took us down... At the door to the gallery, we found ourselves face to face with the Empress, who came forward in the most gracious and charming way. She received us most kindly and was good enough to show us round the gallery herself and point out the finest pictures, saying:

"You will have to make allowances for my gallery, the men are at work there."
"After a quarter of an hour, she withdrew, leaving us delighted with her. I found her much better than I expected, very agreeable, simply but well dressed, with a good figure."

"The gallery was so well built, so well painted and with such taste, so perfectly lighted from above, so well proportioned that one could not hope to see a more beautiful room."

"Among the statues was Canova's delicious *Hebe*, one of his *Cupid and Psyche* groups, etc, etc."

"The paintings are not numerous but very well chosen: four splendid Claude Lorrain's, a painting said to be Teniers' masterpiece, etc, etc. It is the pick of the Cassel Gallery."

26
Pierre-Paul Prud'hon.
Unfinished portrait of the Empress Josephine.

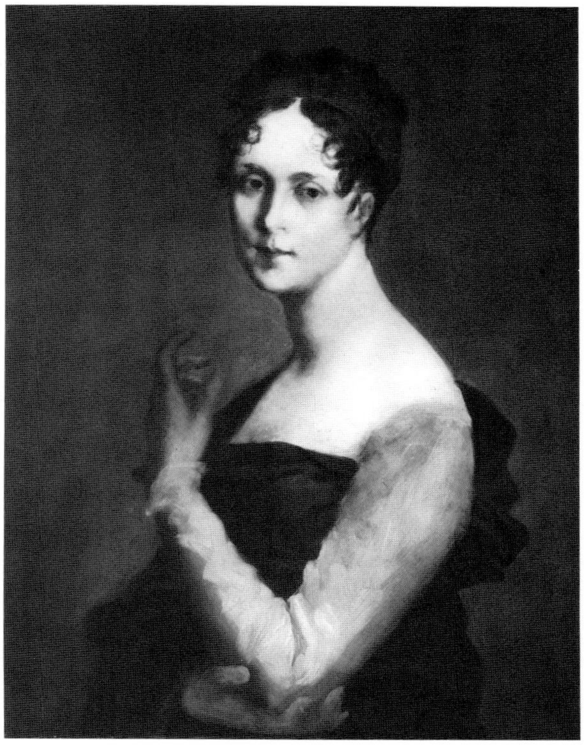

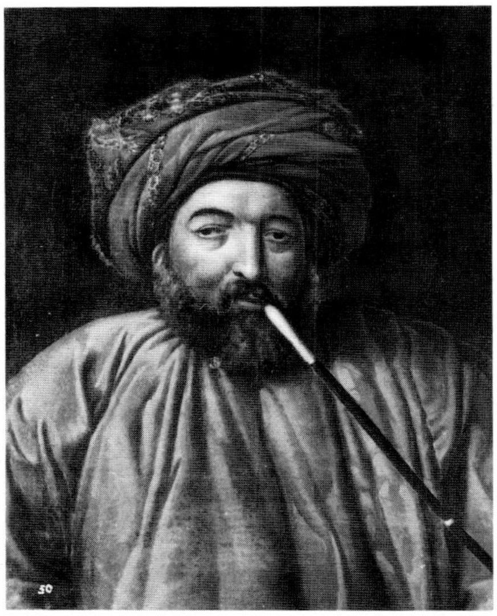

27
Michele Rigo († 1815). Sheik Maalem Guerguis El Geoari, member of the Cairo Divan during the expedition in Egypt.

"The next room contains all the best works of the modern French school, among others: by Richard whom I love, *Valentine of Milan weeping for her husband*, and the same artist's *Charles VII writing on the floor: "Sweet Agnes will remain in my heart longer than the British in our France"*; the *Death of Raphael* with the painting of the Transfiguration at the background, by Laurent (sic, for Bergeret), etc, etc."

"One room if full of splendid heads of Turks. These are the portraits of all those with whom Bonaparte had dealings in Egypt... We saw his books in his little study and the writing-desk from which he had changed and overturned the world by strokes of his pen."

... "The Empress's carriages were ready for an outing. Nothing could be lighter or more elegant. They are open barouches with a huge parasol in the middle; the horses and jockeys are charming."

Mademoiselle Avrillion, first lady of the bedchamber, gives details, confirmed by other witnesses, of small incidents of daily life, in which animals play a large part: ... "At this period, the vestibules at Malmaison were like an aviary; all around them were quantities of bird cages containing the rare birds of which Her Majesty was a great amateur. Among others, she had a charming little parakeet which talked wonderfully, but as she was not a gentle bird, she was not allowed out of her cage."

... "The Empress took pleasure... in visiting the pheasants in her preserve and other animals that had become almost tame. There was a great amount of golden pheasants from China, particularly beautiful. The river was peopled with quantities of all kinds of acquatic birds; but the most curious of all were two beautiful black swans, who had several nests of cygnets; these were the only ones of their kind that had ever become acclimatized in France."

28
Rigo. Sheik Soleyman El Fayoumi.

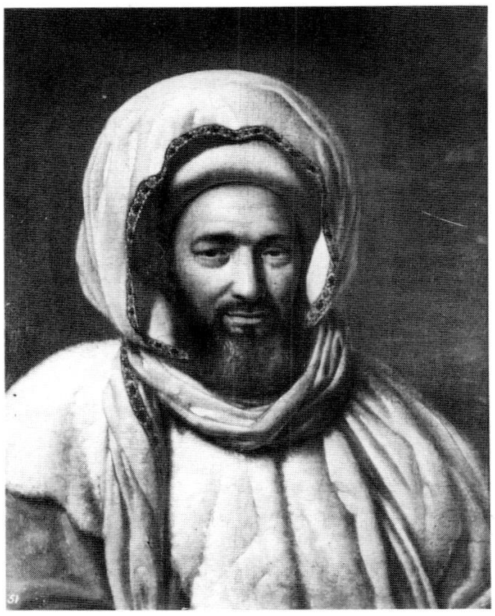

"Her Majesty had a menagery but when the animals it contained died, they were not replaced: for a time she also had several gazelles. These animals were extraordinarily light and graceful, but they lived free and wandered at will in the park at Malmaison. The menagery contained a female monkey of the orang-outang family. The traveller to the Island of France who brought her had given her an excellent education. When anyone approached the chair on which she was seated, it was most curious to see her pull the skirts of her long coat down over her thighs and assume a modest, decent air to welcome the visitor. She ate at table and used a knife and fork skilfully, especially for cutting up turnips, of which she was extremely fond. When she had finished her dinner, one of her chief pleasures was to cover her face with a table-napkin, then to remove it and make all sorts of droll grimaces. One day she fell ill with a rather serious inflamation of the intestins; she was put into a bed, dressed in a nightgown and spencer, just like a woman. She could not bear anything on her head and lay with the cover drawn up to her chin and her arms outside it, completely hidden by the sleeves of the spencer. If anyone she knew came into the room, she greeted him with an appealing look, shaking her head gently and pressing his hand affectionately. It was amusing to see her drink her infusions; as they were sweet, she gulped them greedily. Once, among other medicins, she had to take manna and as the person who nursed her had been ordered to give it only at a certain hour, the animal became impatient and would cry, wriggle about, gesticulate like an angry child, throw the blanket off the bed, pull at her nurse's clothes, until at last the latter was forced to give in and hand her the cup. She would seize this with both hands, sipping and showing the greatest satisfaction, then lie down again very quietly, after returning the cup with a grateful look. Some time after this, the poor beast died."

Josephine now mistress of Malmaison began altering her apartments. The great Ossianian compositions by Gérard and Girodet disappeared from the drawing-room. Above the wainscotting and between the mahogany pilasters, the walls decorated with medallions showing bucolic subjects were painted white with light gilded antique motifs by Delécluze, harmonizing with the new furniture. This comprised two settees, eight armchairs, six X-shaped stools, two small footstools, "all these in wood painted white and gold, covered in petit-point tapestry, embroidered in "passé" stitch" on white ground, with white quinze-seize curtains with gold crests and veilings of embroidered muslin. The room was thus better adapted for its use. The galleries and small chapel nearby were decorated with new statues by Canova, the *Dancer* and the *Pâris* and remained unchanged thereafter. The collection of paintings catalogued in 1811 comprised 252 pictures. By 1814, there were 345. The Council-chamber became a drawing-groom hung with "a striped fabric from India with drapery and fringes", furnished "with a white marble tea-table, with its foot of bronze and gilded copper"... "a pier-table with a mirror at the bottom and green and white marble on top", two writing-desks of mahogany and citron-wood, two day-beds, ten large armchairs, six chairs, ten X-shaped folding stools covered with red cloth as at the time of the Consulate. The bedroom was given the form of an oval tent, with red draperies "embroidered in fine gold", upheld by small columns of gilded wood. In the centre of the ceiling, young Merry-Joseph Blondel painted *Juno in her chariot drawn by white horses.* Jacob Desmalter carved a splendid bed, gilded all over, garnished with red cloth and gold-embroidered muslin. The décor, enriched by the sumptuous silver-gilt toilet-set, was now truly imperial, as Josephine doubtless desired it to be so as to recall the titles she still bore. The other rooms – the bedchamber in ordinary, toilet cabinet, boudoir, bathroom, decorated with mirrors, hung with muslin or "gourgouran" were elegant and refined. Above them was the "wardrobe", where hundreds of gowns, shawls, cashmeres and furs were kept.

Mademoiselle Avrillion gives the exact distribution of the rooms: "After the divorce, Her Majesty slept alone in her bedroom... to reach my own, which was on the same level, one had to

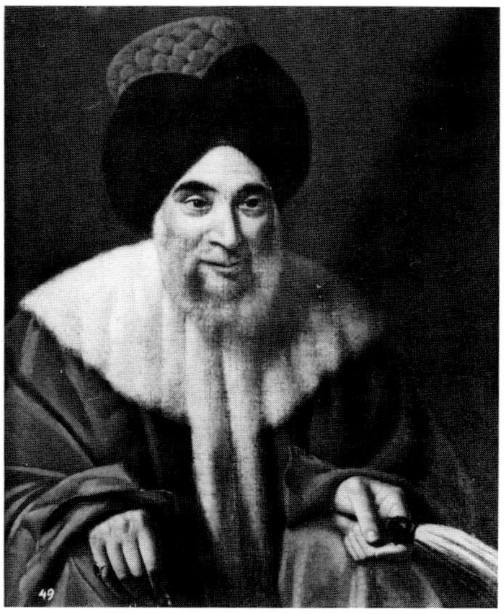

29
Rigo. Sheik Aboul Anouar Al Sadâte, vice-president of the Cairo Divan. Three of the six portraits of Sheiks from the former collection in the château (gift of Empress Eugénie, 1906).

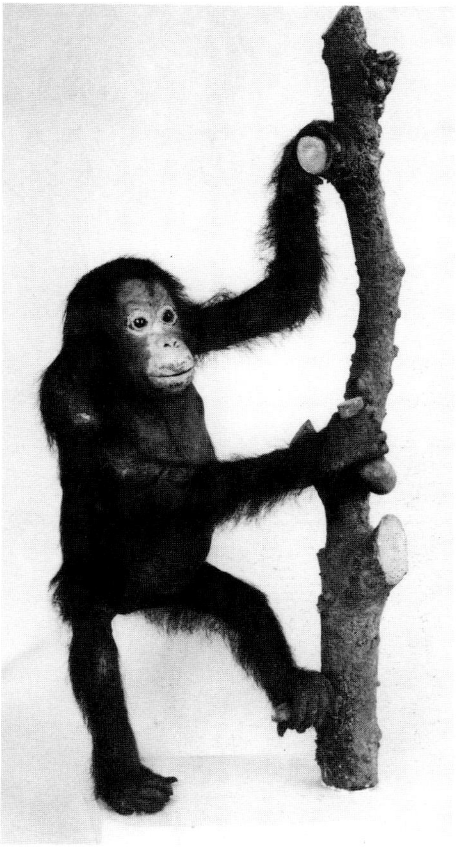

30
Young female orang-outang (pongo pygmaeus), dead at Malmaison, described by Cuvier, naturalized. La Rochelle, Natural History Museum.

31
Court gown, white tulle and silver lamé, having belonged to the Empress and preserved by Queen Hortense (gift Mariano de Unzue, 1927)

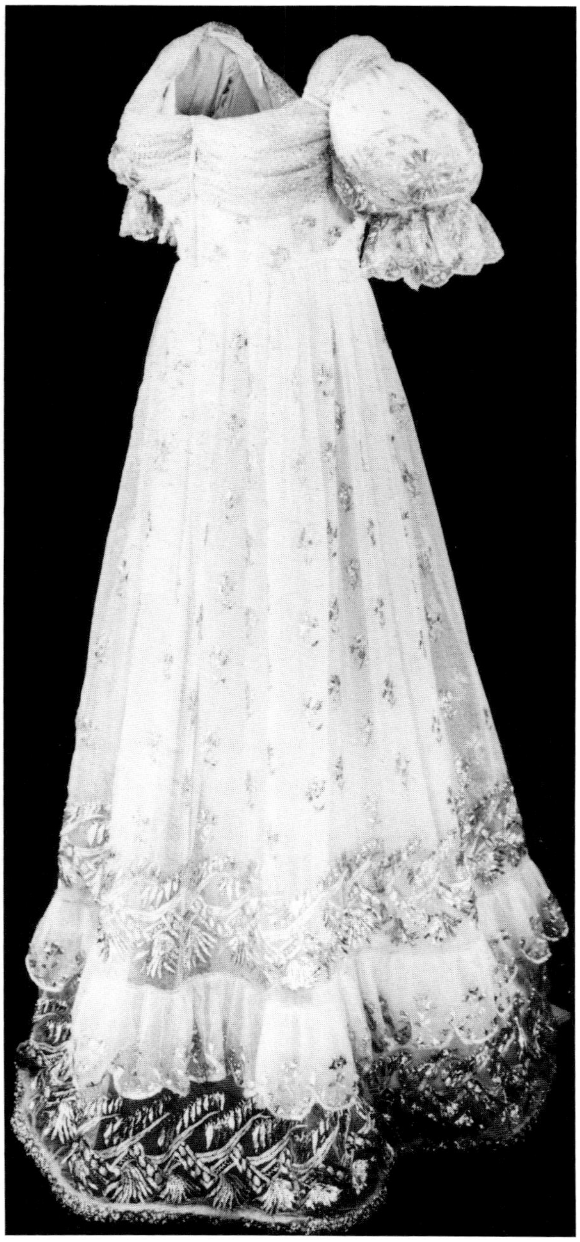

cross an antechamber and a bathroom. Her Majesty would never allow a footman to sleep in the anteroom a night, yet there were no men in the first-floor passage; the gentleman-in-waiting, the chamberlain on duty and Her Majesty's first valet all lodged on the second floor. None of the other men slept in the château; all lodged at Bois-Préau, where they went at night when they came off duty."

The jealousy of Marie-Louise forced Josephine to make long stays at Navarre or to travel in Switzerland or Italy, but during these periods she never forgot her duties as a landowner, finding the upkeep of the domain too expensive, or seeking to embellish it with new buildings for which Cagnola, of Milan, drew up the plans. She was always glad to return to Malmaison, where her interests lay and where she had the advantage of being near Paris. If we are to believe Bourrienne, that old friend grown bitter now, she told him: "Can you imagine what torture it is for me to read all the descriptions of fêtes? And the first time he came to see me after his marriage, what a meeting that was, and what tears it caused me to shed! The days when he comes here are days of torture for me, for he does nothing to spare me. How cruelly he speaks to me of the child he is expecting! Can you understand, Bourrienne, how horrible it is for me? I would sooner be exiled a thousand miles from here." "In reality, Josephine implored Napoleon to visit her, which he did all too rarely, once on June 13th, 1810 and again on January 6th, 1811. However, they continued to write to each other. Josephine longed to see the little King of Rome and caught a glimpse of him at Bagatelle, with the tacit permission of the Emperor.

Bourrienne was nearer the truth when he added: "However, Josephine had such a taste for finery that when she had cried for a quarter of an hour, she would forget her tears to give audience to some fashion-merchant or the inventor of some new kind of ornament. At the sight of a hat, Josephine ceased to be anything but a woman. I remember that one day, when she had been pacified by the arrival of a stock of new finery, I took advantage of the moment to congratulate her on the favourable influence it had on her: "Well, my friend," she said to me, "I ought to be indifferent to all that,but it has become a habit with me." Josephine might have added: and a way of passing the time. It would be no exaggeration to say that if one subtracted from Josephine's life the time she spent in crying and dressing herself up, there would not be much left."

A few months later, the duchesse d'Abrantès remarked: "I found her grown a lot fatter. That did and did not suit her. It suited her face because once a woman is over forty she must get fatter so that her face retains a look of youth... It did not suit her because her exquisite figure had almost disappeared; she had become fat and her waist had that matronly look one sees on the statues of Agrippina, Cornelia, Livia, etc. One part of her person especially had increased to a quite extraordinary extent and her way of dressing, though she had perfect taste, made it look even larger." There follows the description of a morning gown of embroidered muslin.

Her two grandsons made long stays at Malmaison. The younger, nicknamed "Yes-Yes" was to become Napoleon III. She was saddened by the unhappy events of 1812-1813, and the invasion of 1814, and she encouraged her son Eugène to remain faithful. The advance of the allied troops forced her to leave Malmaison on March 29th and take refuge at Navarre, where she learned of the abdication and the return of the Bourbons. What would become of her and her children? The question was decided by the treaty of April 11th. She considered for a moment joining Napoleon in the island of Elba. She returned to Malmaison on April 15th. Next day, there was a visit from the Tzar Alexander who had taken her under his protection. Hortense notes: "I arrived at Malmaison at one o'clock. I was astonished to see the courtyard full of cossacks and great activity everywhere, and I asked the reason. I was told that my mother was walking in the garden with the Emperor of Russia. I went to join them and met them near the hot-house. My mother was pleased and surprised to see me. She kissed me tenderly and said to the Emperor: "Here is my daughter with my grandsons. I recommend them to you." On the same day, Napoleon wrote to her from Fontainebleau. It was to be his last letter!

The King of Prussia, the German princes, the grand-dukes, followed the Tzar's example to such an extent that the Bourbons became alarmed at such friendship.

In a letter to his sister Sophia, dated April 25th, the future Leopold I of Belgium, who had taken service with Russia after renouncing that of France, wrote: "This evening, I am to dine with the Grand-Duke at Malmaison; I hope you will be pleased with me when you read the following: though everyone loves poor Josephine and Queen Hortense, they are in a very difficult position. Though they asked nothing of me, I have been looking after them and I arranged an interview with the "César" at Malmaison which had the happiest consequences for them. There was no-one but me who could talk to the Emperor on this subject, and I did not hesitate to make things right for them. Now, I can congratulate myself on this point. They were very friendly to me at the time of their prosperity, and now that nobody cares about them and I can no longer hope for any protection from them, I have acted in such a way as to show them my gratitude and have protected them in my turn."

On May 14th, Hortense, accompanied by her mother and Prince Eugène, received Alexander at Saint-Leu, at his own request. While out walking, Josephine caught cold. On May 23rd, she had a visit from the King of Prussia and the Grand-Duke Constantine. "My mother was already ill and made an effort to come down to welcome them. She seemed to me to have a mere cold and her health was usually so good that I was not at all worried. On May 24th, she had to keep to her bed. Her doctor, Dr. Horeau, did not seem worried. On the 27th: "The Emperor of Russia sent his chief doctor. Though she was very tired, she said to him in her usual gracious way: "Please thank the Emperor of Russia. I hope his interest will bring me luck."

"The Emperor Alexander was to come to dinner next

32
Double-faced mirror, mahogany and bronze gilt, by Biennais.

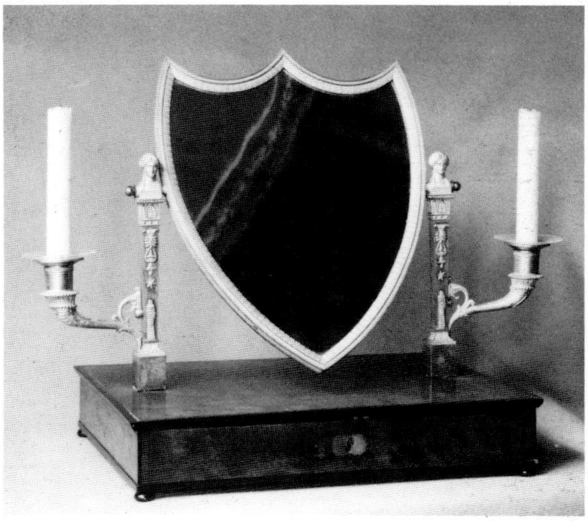

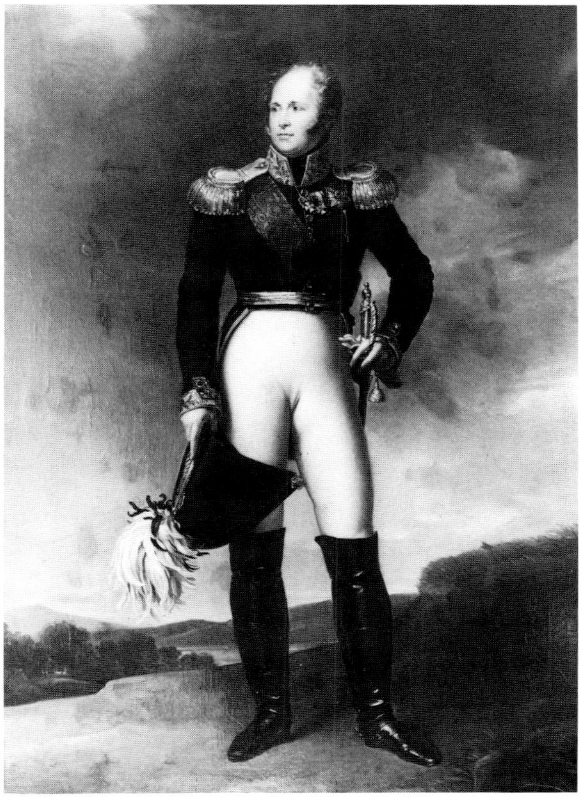

33
François Gérard (1770-1837) Tzar Alexander I of Russia (gift of Princess George of Greece and Denmark, 1959).

day. She supervised every detail for his reception and intended to get up to welcome him. When he left her, the doctor's anxious face prepared us for what he had to say: he found her very ill."

"Terrified, I sent for the best doctors in Paris", Bourdois, Lamoureux and Lasserre."

The 28th: "I was about to beg the Emperor to put off the dinner till another day, when he arrived very early. I received him, told him of my fears and took him to see my brother, where we all agreed to hide his presence from my mother who would become agitated if she thought he was not getting a proper welcome. I went back to her and told her that he had sent excuses and would come to dinner another day. "I am sure," she said "that he is embarrassed because he has no news about your brother and does not like to come without it." I assured her that our affairs would turn out well. She repeated several times: "We must risk talking to the Emperor of Russia about your brother, since he is the only one on our side. Should we let him go without anything being decided?" I promised her... I went continually between my mother's room and that of my brother, where the Emperor, who stayed till evening, was sitting with him."

"I stayed late with my mother. I brought my children to wish her goodnight. She sent them away at once, saying: "The air here is bad; it might harm them". She wanted to send me away too. I got up twice but stayed near my mother's apartment. My waiting-woman told me not to worry, that she was peaceful, though she sometimes murmured a few words: "Bonaparte... island of Elba... the King of Rome."

Next day, May 29th, which was Whitsunday, my brother, who had left his bed in spite of his fever, came with me early in the morning to my mother's room. When she saw us, she held out her arms with great emotion and uttered something we could not understand."

At eleven o'clock, Josephine received the Sacraments, administered by Abbé Bertrand. By midday, she was dead. Noone thought of informing Bonaparte, who learned the news from a newspaper sent from Genoa to the island of Elba! Louis XVIII was informed through the police journal he received every morning. "Madame de Beauharnais' death is regretted by everyone. This woman had an inborn gentleness and something attractive and elegant in both mind and manners... During her husband's reign she endured great sadness and took refuge from his brutality and contempt in botanical culture... The public knew how she struggled to save the victims of Bonaparte and was grateful to her for having embraced his knees in the hope of saving the duc d'Enghien." The death-certificate was cunningly worded and mentioned, "The Empress Josephine, née Marie Joséphine Rose Tacher de la Pagerie, married to Napoleon Bonaparte, General-in-chief of the Army in Italy..."

The funeral took place on June 2nd in the church at Rueil. A Russian detachment paid her a last tribute. Alexander was represented by his aide-de-camp, General Osten-

Sacken, Governor of Paris. Hortense and Eugène had retired, broken-hearted, to Saint-Leu. Hortense's sons, both of them still children, led their grandmother's funeral procession. Mgr de Barral, Archbishop of Tours and head-chaplain to the Empress, pronounced a tactful funeral oration. The attendance was considerable and regrets unanimous.

34
Water-colour plan of the châteaux and parks of Malmaison and Bois-Préau, about 1815.

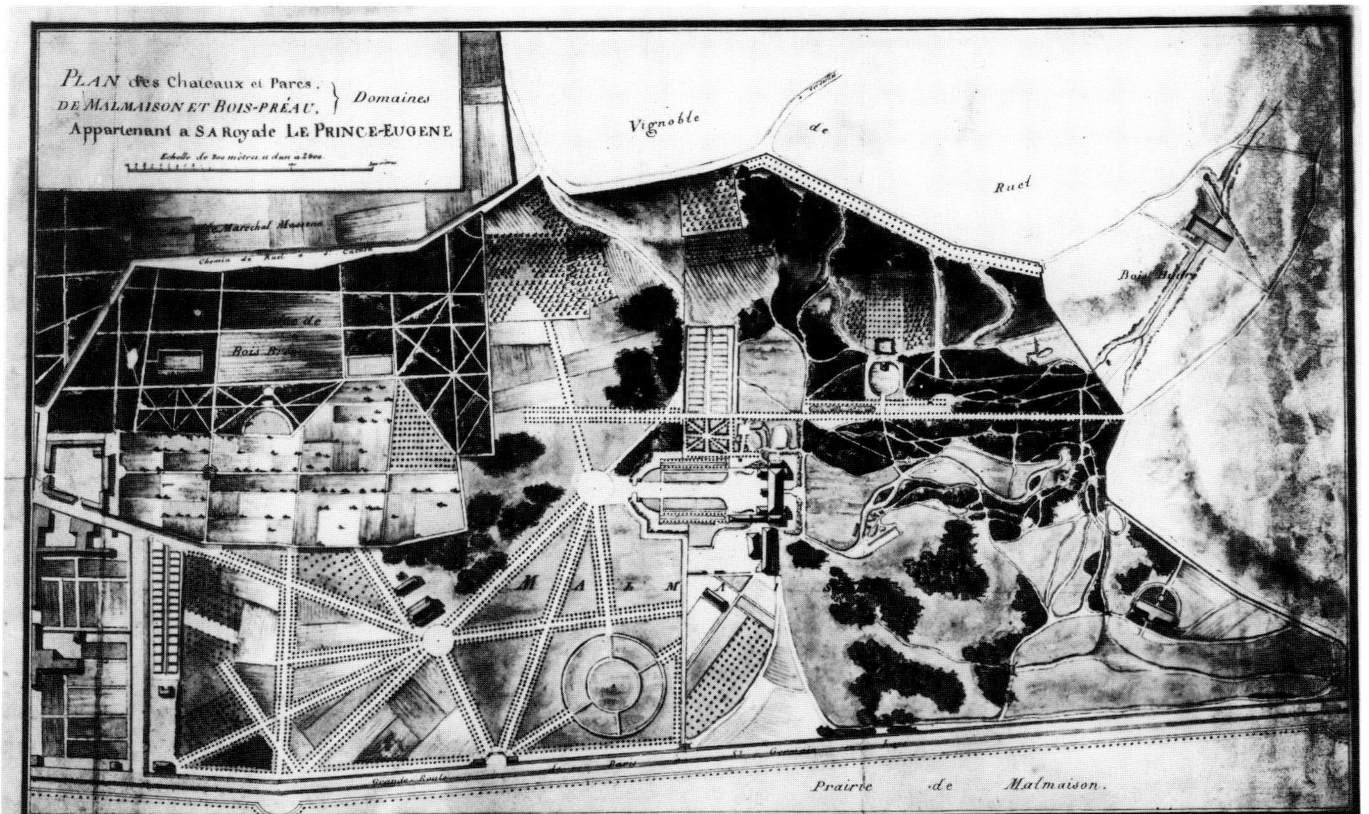

Malmaison after Josephine

35
Jean-Baptiste Regnault (1754-1829). Queen Hortense, signed portrait
(gift of Mrs Helen Fahnestock-Hubbard, 1927).

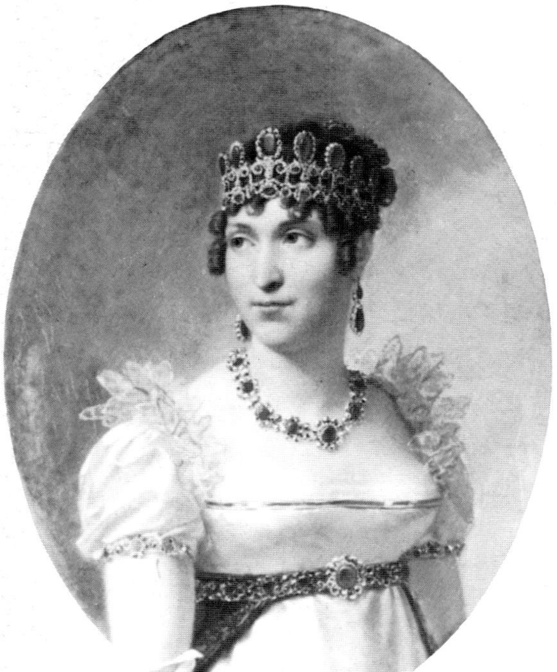

The new monarchic government did nothing to facilitate a succession encumbered with a debt of three million francs. The situation of the heirs — Eugène, Napoleon's adopted son, and Hortense, separated but not divorced from Louis Bonaparte and thus both the Emperor's step-daughter and sister-in-law — was obscure. Maître André-Claude Noël, successor to Raguideau, the imperial notary, had inventories of Malmaison and Bois-Préau drawn up on June 8th, in presence of Eugène and Hortense's agents, the Chevalier Soulange-Bodin and Baron Devaux. The operation lasted forty-two days. Jewels, silverware, furs, cashmeres, gowns, furniture, paintings, statues, art objects, books, not to mention the animals, rare plants, fine wines and various materials were patiently recorded and numbered from one to 2916. Hortense got the jewels, some of the modern paintings and the two small châteaux of La Chaussée and Prégny, but the greater part went to Eugène, with the chief domain covering 726 hectares, most of the furniture and works of art. The most important paintings, notably those from the Cassel Gallery and Canova's statues, were immediately and discretely ceded to the Tzar Alexander for a sum of about a million francs. Malmaison was not, however, entirely unfurnished when Napoleon, having escaped from the island of Elba, returned in triumph to Paris on March 20th 1815. Prince Eugène, now Duke of Leuchtenberg, remained prudently in Bavaria, but Hortense, created Duchess of Saint-Leu by Louis XVIII, was present. She was pardoned and held court for the Emperor, now abandoned by Marie-Louise and deprived of his son, who was kept in Vienna.

On April 11th, Napoleon sent the Grand-Marshal Bertrand, to ask Hortense to receive him for lunch at Malmaison the next morning. "He sent me a list of people he desired to meet there. I admit I found it hard to do the honours for him in a place I had left at the saddest moment of my life and that I had not had the courage to visit since. As I feared the impression would be too painful and wanting to see it first without witnesses, I went to Malmaison the very evening... I became calmer during the night and next day I prepared to receive the Emperor without seeming too much upset. He arrived at 9 o'clock; he was obviously moved; we walked everywhere together and at each moment he exclaimed: "How all these spots remind me of her! I cannot believe she is no longer here." After lunch, he got into a carriage with me, M. Molé and M. Denon. He wanted to talk to the latter about some art objects. The other guests followed in other carriages. We went a long way and talked of a thousand things."

"Before he left, he received the notables of Rueil and the parish priest... As he was about to enter his carriage, the Emperor wanted to see the room where my mother had died: "Stay here", he said to me, "it would be too painful for you." When he returned, he seemed greatly affected."

After Waterloo and the second abdication, Napoleon took refuge at Malmaison. On the evening of June 24th, Hortense was at the Elysée: "The Emperor... said to me: "Malmaison belongs to you; I should like to go there and I should be very pleased if you would stay with me. I will go tomorrow, but I do not want to occupy the Empress's apartment." I showed that I was pleased to be of use to him and I went to arrange for my departure."

"I left next day with Mme d'Arjuzon, after hiding my children in the homes of reliable people, so that I should have nothing to do but look after the Emperor. I arranged the whole of one side of the château for him... and I kept the other side, which contained the Empress's apartment, for myself and those who accompanied us. I had the small gallery arranged as a dining-room where I should dine with all the people who accompanied him. He arrived in the morning" (actually, early in the afternoon).

"That very evening, the Emperor's brothers, the Duke of Bassano, M. Lavalette, came to see him; I stayed in the drawing-room with all the officers of his household and my own; we thought of nothing but how we could save him. The young officers... insisted that the royalists would come to take him and they prepared to defend him. We did not go to bed. Thirty men of the Dragoons of the Guard, who had remained behind, still suffering from their wounds and half armed, M.M. Gourgaud, de Montholon, de Montaron, the aide-de-camp on duty and M. de Las Cases, the chamberlain, four orderly officers and the young page Sainte-Catherine d'Audiffredi, a young American related to my mother, M. de Marmol, my equerry, such was our military strength." The Queen forgot her grenadiers and foot soldiers in the Rueil barracks, some 300 men! "I retired late with Mme d'Arjuzon; all the men stayed on the watch."

"Next day... (June 26th) the Emperor sent for me at ele-

36
Alexandre and Alix Sainte-Catherine d'Audiffredi, young relations of the Empress. Miniature
(Bequest of Mme Lecuyer, 1949).

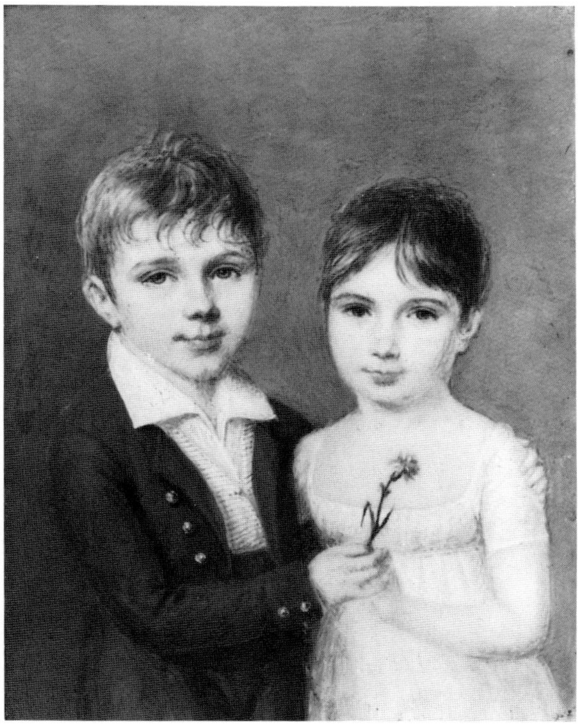

ven o'clock; he was walking alone in the garden;.. the weather was splendid... He said to me, with a touching look, "That poor Josephine! I can't get used to being here without her! I keep thinking I see her come from one of the alleys and pick these plants she loved so much! Poor Josephine!" Then, seeing my sadness, he added: "Actually, she would be miserable now. We only quarrelled on one subject: her debts and I scolded her a lot. I never knew anyone so full of grace. She was a woman in every sense of the word, changeable, lively and with the best of hearts. Have another portrait of her done for me. I should like it to be a medallion." I promised him."

"The Emperor's brothers arrived with his mother, who seemed very depressed. I drew King Joseph aside and begged him once more to urge the Emperor to take a decision. He merely said: "You are right", and I retired..."

37
Joseph Chinard (1756-1813). Empress Josephine, bust, marble, signed, 1805-1806
(gift of Empress Eugénie).

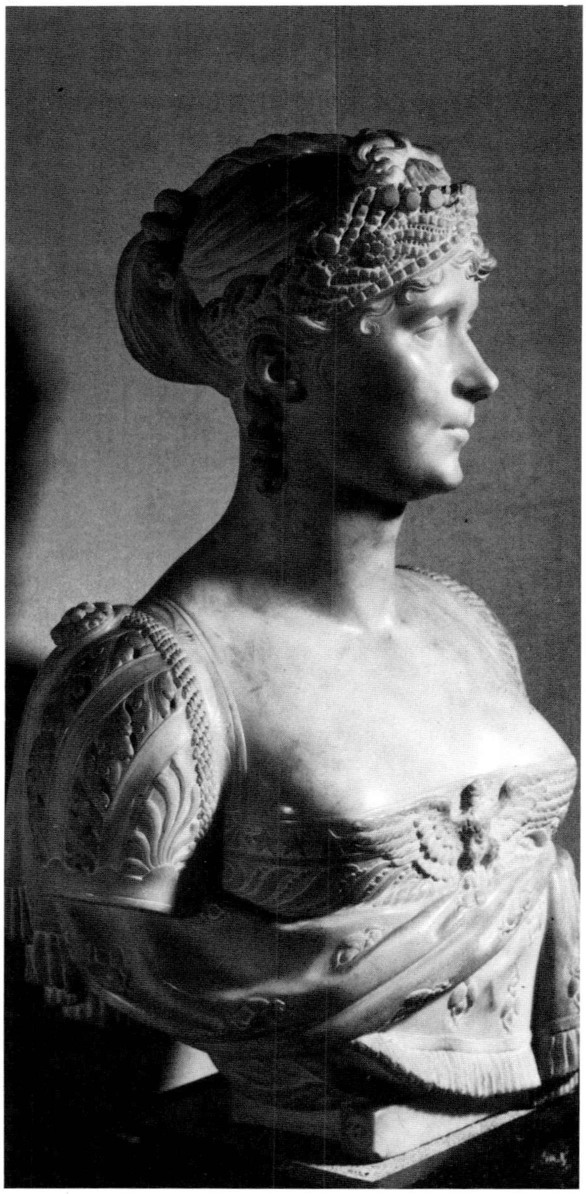

"I found M.M. de Flahaut, de la Bédoyère and the duc de Rovigo in the drawing-room and they told me Paris was quiet, there were merely a few royalists carrying their heads high. A moment later, a man came to tell the duc de Rovigo of the plot formed by five hundred royalists to assassinate the Emperor the next night, while the duchesse de Rovigo, who had arrived from Paris, had met several men on horseback near Malmaison, among them one of her cousins, a fervent royalist. These pieces of news were brought to the Emperor, who paid no attention to them. Towards evening, our young men, who had spent the day in Paris, began again to prepare for an attack... We heard a pistol shot; everyone was on the alert, except the Emperor, who did not seem to notice it... Perhaps the provisional Government, anxious to get the Emperor away, had wanted to frighten him? This event was never explained."

"We were constantly on the look-out, but as our army drew nearer to Paris, the royalists began to tremble and there was less danger of an attack on Malmaison. In the evening, the Emperor received an officer who came to beg him, in the name of the Army, to take command of the troops once more. I don't know if the provisional Government knew of this, but next day (in reality, on the evening of June 25th) he sent General Beker to take command of our guardsmen..."

"However, my fears for the Emperor were somewhat appeased when I learned that two frigates were waiting at the port of La Rochelle (*sic*, for Rochefort). A difficulty arose then: the provisional Government wished him to go there at once, and he desired first to be sure the ships would take the direction he wished. M. de Flahaut was sent to Paris to discuss the matter and he had a violent scene with the Prince d'Eckmuhl, the Minister for War. The departure was again delayed by this argument over the frigates. I felt each day diminished the chances of escaping the English. I tried again with King Joseph, who was the one who talked most frequently with the Emperor."

Hortense evokes the presence at Malmaison of other visitors, notably that of little Léon, who knew nothing of his origins ("Hortense, look at that child: who is he like?" "He is your son, Sire, he's the portrait of the King of Rome" — "You think so? then it must be true. I did not think I was softhearted but I was moved when I saw him"), the Countess Walewska, Mme Duchatel, but she neglects Napoleon's conversations with the treasurer Peyrusse, the banker Laffitte, the notary Noël.

"M. Gabriel Delessert came from Paris to tell me that one of General Exelmans' aides-de-camp, who had been at the front, thought the enemy was making a movement in direction of Saint-Germain, doubtless with a view to cutting off the Emperor's retreat. He was in his study; I went in to tell him M. Delessert's news and he sent for him and asked him in my presence for some further explanations. On his table was a large map, on which he stuck pins to mark the position of the various corps. He changed some of these in accordance with what M. Delessert had told him; he asked him the number of enemy troops encircling Paris and, on M. Delessert's reply, he cried: "Poor Paris! To be taken by a handful of Prussians!"

Hortense continues the detailed account of these crucial days, with a few chronological errors, corrected by other witnesses or participants in the events. On Wednesday, June 28th, "I offered him my travelling carriage, but he refused, preferring to leave in a barouche. He asked what I meant to do and what my fortune amounted to. I told him I had only my diamonds and those of my mother, because the succession had all gone to pay off old debts, but that I should retire to Switzwerland... I told him he might need to take some diamonds with him and that he could have mine, that he had given them to me and they belonged to him. He consented to take a string worth two hundred thousand francs and insisted on writing me a recognition for them... Then he told me for the first time of his plans, saying he would go to the United States and that those who bore his name would have no choice but to rejoin him there..."

"Then we heard cries coming from the main road... we saw hundreds of soldiers gazing at Malmaison and throwing their caps in the air, crying: *Long live the Emperor!* They were sent in the direction of Saint-Germain... The Emperor seemed touched: "It is not cries but acts I need," he said and he quickly returned to his study. His mother and family came to say goodbye to him..."

"Madame Bertrand had been making arrangements to leave with her husband in the suite of the Emperor, and she now arrived from Paris. She insisted, with her usual vivacity, that the Emperor ought to take refuge in England, where he would find a warm welcome. She went to see him in his study... We walked together all evening, Mme Bertrand and myself. The weather was splendid... We had been sitting for a time on a bench and discussing our ideas when we saw the Emperor himself coming to join us. He seemed to share the peace awoken in our hearts by the calm of all nature, for he sat down beside us and exclaimed: "How beautiful Malmaison is! Hortense, would we not be happy to stay here?" I could not reply; my voice would have betrayed my emotion. This was the first time he seemed to have become fond of a place and I was all the more surprised because I had believed him incapable of such a feeling."

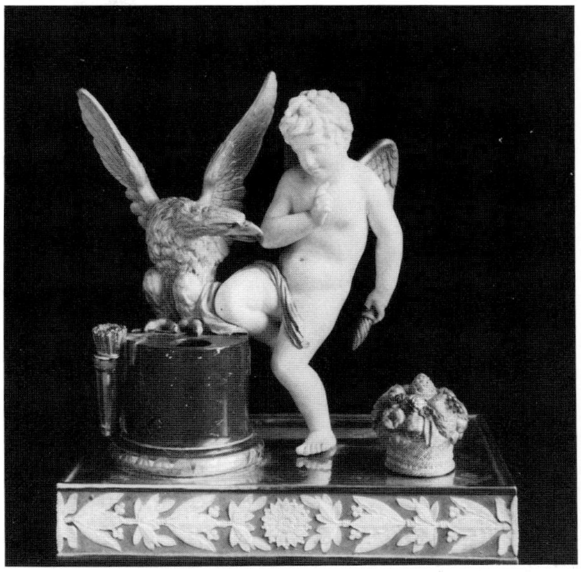

38
Cupid playing with an eagle, inkstand in Paris porcelaine, Dagoty manufactory.

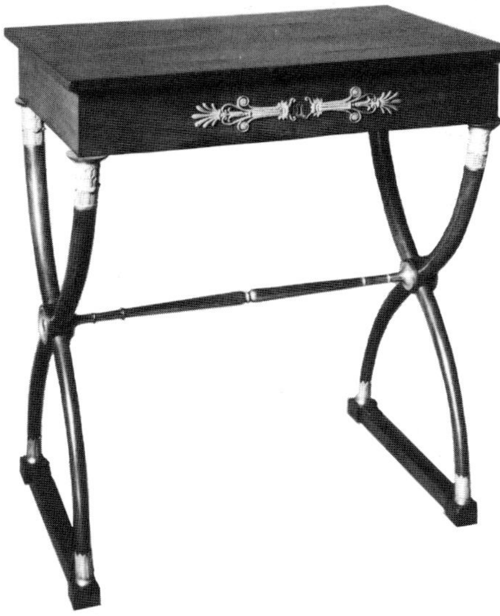

39
Writing-table, mahogany and gilded bronzes. The lid can be raised to reveal an inkstand, pen-holder and desk.

"The evening passed as the previous ones had done. We stayed in the drawing-room discussing the Emperor's journey with the people who were to accompany him, while he stayed in his study with the Duc de Bassano."

Before going to bed at eleven o'clock, Napoleon sent for Frère, Josephine's head valet, now in service with Prince Eugène, who immediately after noted down his remarks in a touchingly racy and clumsy style. The Emperor, as usual, asked some questions about the staff and the domain, taking an interest in everything...

- "Malmaison is a lovely place.
- Yes, Sire, it's fine...
- Everything here reminds me of that poor Josephine... You stayed with Her all the time?"
- I left Her only in her tomb...
(The Emperor had got into bed)
- ... All these apartments (speaking of the room where he slept) aren't what they were in my time?
- This room isn't really the thing for your Majesty.
- I didn't want to sleep in that poor Josephine's room...
- ...
- Ah, yes, it is very fine, Malmaison. It is a lovely place; but Josephine spent a lot and there's no house; I was always on at her, wasn't I?
- That's true, Sire.
- But it's very lovely.
- Yes, Sire, and if we'd only finished what She began before She died...
- What?
- That alley you must have noticed near your little garden, for going to Boispréau.
- What's Boispréau?
- It's Mlle Julien's park.
- Ah, yes... Oh, we must finish that.
- The Empress was full of it and it gave work to a lot of poor peasants.
- Josephine didn't leave you anything?
- She didn't leave a will, but the Queen and the Prince give me a pension of 1,500 francs.
- What's happened to the porter, an old sergeant?
- ...
(I thought the Emperor had gone to sleep and I was on my way out; I was really touched.)
- Are the people in Rueil fair to us?
- Yes, Sire, they were very fond of the Empress.
- She spent a lot here?
- Yes, Sire, she gave a lot of work to people.
- Ah! She spent more than she had... She wanted everything.
- ...
- Are there still sheep here?
- Yes, Sire.
- Josephine thought that splendid.
- ...
- Josephine is in the church at Rueil?

JOSEPHINE'S TOMB

My friends, in this village,
We keep the coffin
Of a sweet and wise woman
Mourned by the whole universe.
You shall hear the misfortunes
Of this heavenly woman.
(chorus)

On Josephine's tomb
Come, come to shed your tears.
(bis)

This good Empress
Brought much happiness
And her consoling voice
Cheered the wretches.
Around her, orphans
Forgot their sorrow.
(chorus)

She honoured science,
Rewarded virtue,
And by her virile eloquence
Abolished wrongs.
She was gay and playful,
Refusing flattery.
(chorus)

A dread destiny
Led her spouse to desert her.
In a humble refuge,
Without grandeur, she expired.
This loss afflicts us.
Our hearts are full of regret.
(chorus)

- Yes, Sire.
- Have they given her a monument?
- Not yet, Sire, there's an estimate for a fine mausoleum, but the circumstances haven't been right, we were waiting for the Prince. The Empress is in a chapel hung all in black, since last year, and they say Masses for her...
"I thought I saw the Emperor fall asleep and I retired."
"On leaving, I went to Queen Hortense and told her about this conversation and after I went up to my room and put it all down on paper just as I kept it all fresh in my head."

Hortense is the main witness of Napoleon's farewell to Malmaison. Thursday, June 29th, "Everything is ready for the departure. King Joseph arrived early; he was shut up with the Emperor when Rousseau, my head valet, brought me a letter from Paris... the enemy was believed to be already at Malmaison... the Neuilly bridge was already barricaded... I hurried into the Emperor's study to bring him this news. He heard it very cooly and said... that it would be wise for me to return to Paris with the other ladies: "Sire," I said, "I am only worried about you..." — "My girl," he said to me, "We know what war is. Go home quickly and take Madame Bertrand with you, for I can't do anything with her husband as long as she is here."

... "He called M. de Résigny, the orderly officer, and sent him to reconnoitre and find out how far away was the enemy."

"MM. de Flahaut and Lavalette arrived from Paris and confirmed the news I had brought him. Then, as if the approach of the enemy led him to think of nothing but the danger to France, he said these exact words, in front of me, to these two gentlemen...; "Go to the provisional Governement and say that I can still hold the army, I can stop the enemy advance and give the Government time to lay down terms in the interests of France and negociate with the allied sovereigns the rights and the liberty she will lose. I promise, on my faith as a general, a citizen and a soldier, to leave the same day that I succeed in freeing the capital." After these words, he dismissed them."

Résigny returned: he had seen the Chatou bridge blown up by Davout's order: "We saw it burning through the windows and that proved the enemy was really there."

"The post-horses arrived, to my great satisfaction, and at the moment when I thought the Emperor was about to leave at last, he would not think of doing so. He was impatient for a reply from the provisional Government and he had enough influence over General Beker, who was in charge of him, to persuade him to accept the same mission he had given to MM. de Flahaut and Lavalette. This delay distressed me greatly for I felt sure the proposals would be refused and the danger was growing hourly. I brought him the diamond necklace he had consented to receive and that I had had arranged and sewn into a ribbon so that it could be worn as a belt, and I tied it round him myself. The valet Marchand had prepared a small phial of poison.

"M. de Flahaut was announced; he had come to report the failure of his mission. The Emperor said: "Why wouldn't they

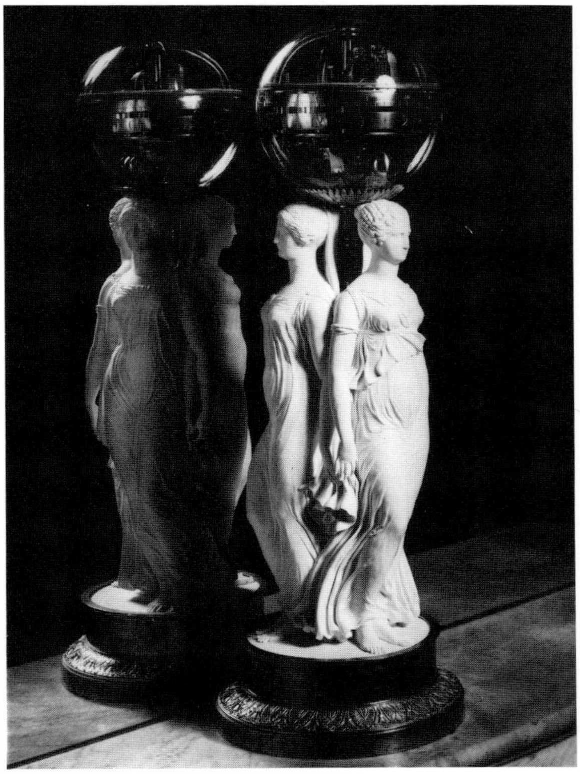

40
Three Graces clock. Group in Sèvres biscuit-ware after Chaudet, movement by Lepaute.

41
Opera-glass and its case with Josephine's monogram, bearing the mark of the optician Lerebours
(gift of comte Roger Walewski, 1960).

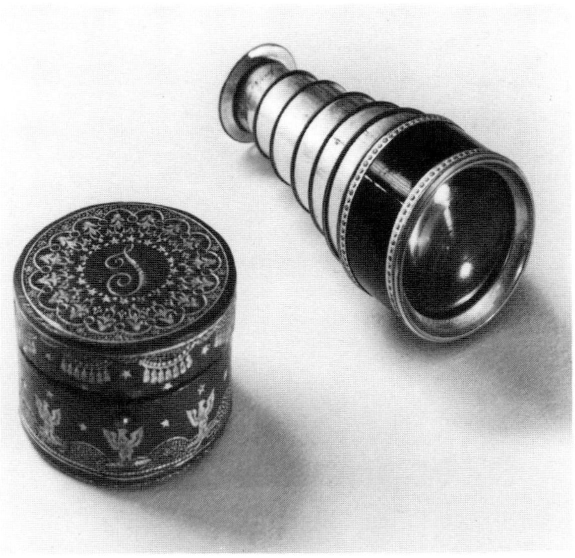

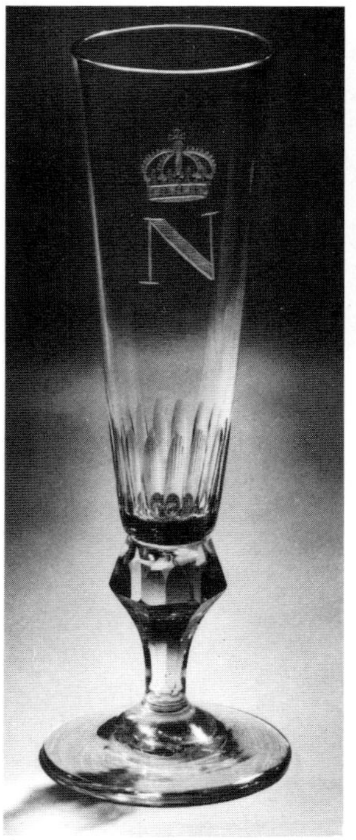

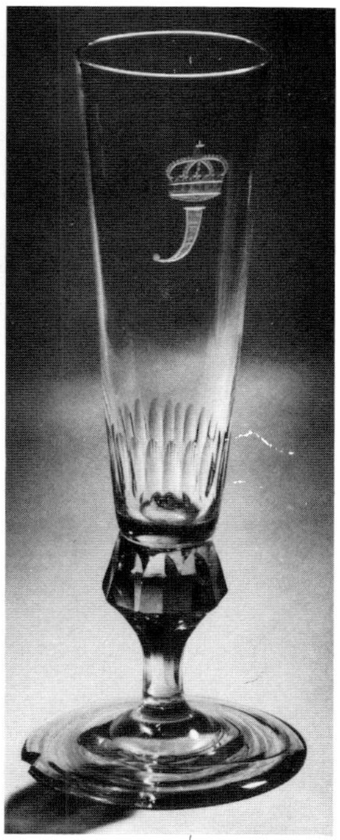

42
Crystal champagne-glass engraved with Napoleon's monogram
(gift of colonel Jourdan, 1938).

43
Crystal champagne-glass engraved with Josephine's monogram
(gift of Empress Eugénie).

44
Small liqueur carafe, engraved with Josephine's monogram (gift of Empress Eugénie).

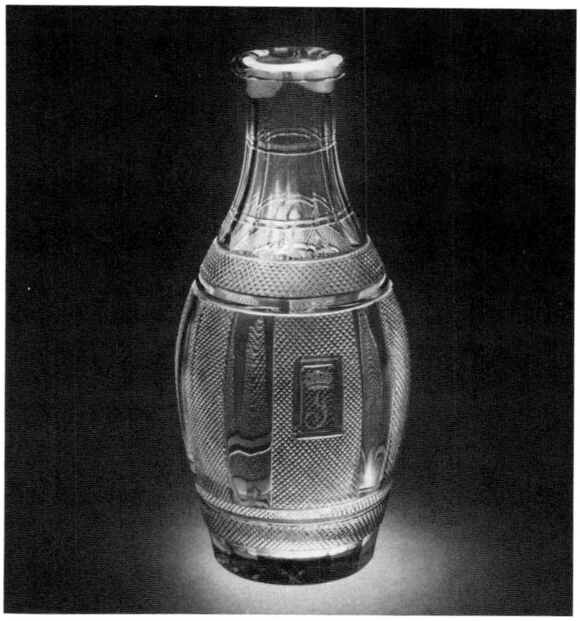

accept? They're still afraid of me, are they?" Flahaut replied that the heads of the Government feared that his person would be an obstacle to negociations and make the adversary doubt their sincerity, but he added that he thought the Government also feared to see the Emperor once more at the head of his Army, in case he refused to leave it: "Did you repeat the promise I made to leave Paris as soon as I had freed it?" — "Yes, Sire." Then the Emperor rose with a determined movement and said: "They refuse. Very well, let us go. I have nothing to reproach myself with. I shall have done my duty to the last. I hoped to make a last effort to save France and she is to be thrown on the mercy of her enemies."

"I kissed him, with tears in my eyes."

"The Emperor passed these last minutes shut up with his brother Joseph. He had taken off his uniform and was wearing a grey morning-coat [dark brown according to Montholon, brown according to Beker]. General Beker came back from Paris, bringing the same reply as M. de Flahaut, and, as we were waiting only for him, the carriages were brought up. The Emperor had with him in his barouche General Beker, General Bertrand and the duc de Rovigo. Colonel Gourgaud, MM. de Montholon, de Las Cases and Lallemand [the latter had left alone from Paris and rejoined them at Niort] were in another carriage. The others... went by a different route." It was five in the afternoon. After a final stage on French territory, at the Ile d'Aix, Napoleon gave himself up to British honour.

With these farewells, Malmaison's great history comes to an end. Henceforth, there will be nothing more to preserve, apart from the memory of the stirring or cruel hours spent there by Napoleon or Josephine.

"Before returning to Paris, I crossed the lovely Malmaison gallery where were kept all the art objects which, together with my diamonds, were now the whole of my fortune. I thought then, for the first time, that my children would possess nothing else... the allies were too near for me to have all those paintings removed to Paris; I bravely made up my mind that they would be lost if fate so decreed it, and I hurried to rejoin my children."

Blucher at once had Malmaison occupied, but the Prussians committed only a few small thefts. When Napoleon learned at St. Helena of the partial sales of art objects carried out during the following years, he "was furious", according to the mameluck Ali: "Is it possible that Eugène, my adopted son, should dirty his hands by making money from the precious objects in the château? Did I not make him rich enough for such baseness to be unnecessary? It would have been fitting, it would have been noble for Eugène to offer them in homage to France and the Paris museum would have been recompensed to some extent for its losses in 1815... Now I suppose he will do the same for Malmaison. There are many reasons why he should love it and hold it sacred; he ought to leave it to his children..."

Eugène died in 1824, leaving children under age. A new inventory was drawn up. His widow, the Princess of Bavaria, decided to sell Malmaison and commissioned the painter Loeillot to make water-colour paintings of the main rooms for her to keep as souvenirs. She had Josephine's bed and a few precious pieces of furniture removed to Munich. With some courage, the notary Casimir Noël drew up and had lithographed a poster advertising "the splendid domain of Malmaison, once the home of Napoleon and Josephine"... "It is the permanent witness to the memorable events which have rendered famous the end of the last century and the beginning of the present." The royal family and the duke of Orléans having refused it, the Swedish banker Jonas Hagerman finally bought it on September 16th 1828, after a great deal of bargaining, for the capital sum of 1,800,000 F. The sale of paintings, books and objects not subject to reserve, took place from May 31st to June 16th, 1829. A few faithful friends, some Englis« hmen and Hagerman himself, bought the greater part. Madame Hagerman and her daughter installed themselves in Josephine's apartment, but made only short stays at Malmaison. When she paid a semi-clandestine visit to Paris in 1831, Queen Hortense was refused an entry. When Hagerman died in 1839, the Great Gallery, theatre and kitchens had already been demolished, and the hot-house transformed into apartments. On May 7th 1842, Malmaison became the property of Ferdinand Muñoz y Sanchez, duke of Riansarès, morganatic husband of Marie-Christine de Bourbon, Queen-regent, then dowager of Spain. The domain was sold for 254,000 F, cut up and reduced to a tenth of its surface. The Queen built a neo-Gothic chapel (demolished in 1912) on the site of the former theatre. As an admirer of Napoleon she respected the décor of the ground floor and planted opposite the entrance a flower-bed in the form of the star of the Legion of Honour, ornamented at the centre with the imperial monogram. In 1843, the nurseryman Béluze christened "Souvenir of Malmaison", in memory of Josephine, a pale, flesh-coloured rose, exquisitely scented, now very rare. During the first years of the Second Empire, Napoleon III and Eugénie sometimes came over as neighbours from Saint-Cloud. The Marquise de la Tour-Maubourg, a lady-in waiting, recalls these summer visits: "One greets the Queen with one's best curtsey; though she is short and too fat, she has a grand air and seems majestic and a bit stiff rather than gracious... we followed their Majesties for a walk in the park and though we noticed a great many roses, there was not one of the kind called Malmaison"...

"When the duc de Rianzarès, the Queen's husband, is there, he is very amiable, showing the apartments on the first floor and doing the honours in a way the Queen cannot do because of her corpulence. Their children are seldom seen; they are very much afraid of the Queen".

On April 15th, 1861, the Emperor bought Malmaison for one million F, remembering how he had often stayed there as a child with his grandmother and sucked sugar-canes. He ordered extensive work on it. Empress Eugénie fitted up in 1867 a museum of souvenirs, and the catalogue, drawn up by Maxime de Lescure, shows that part of the furniture and some portraits were back in their old places.

BAVIERE
1824-1828

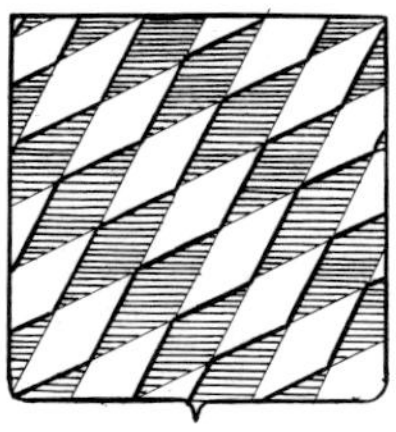

MUNOZ
1842-1861

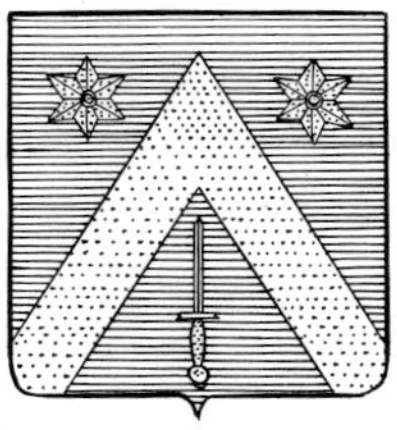

45
Snuffbox in chased gold and enamel, with the mark of the goldsmith Marguerite, decorated with miniature-portraits of Josephine, Louis Bonaparte, Hortense and Eugène de Beauharnais, by Isabey. Napoleon took it with him to St. Helena and bequeathed it to his son.

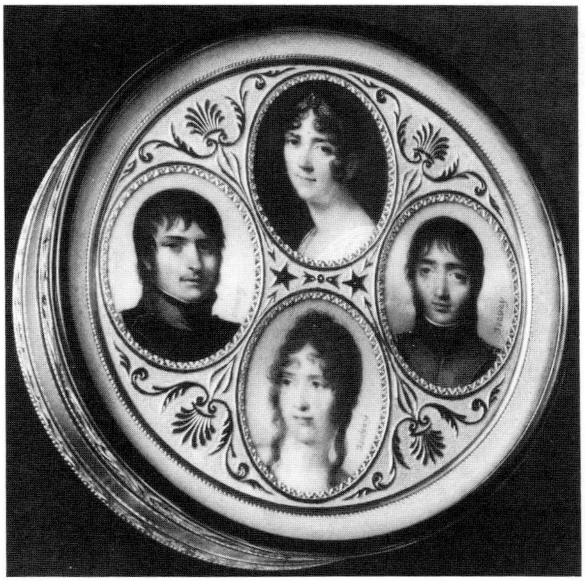

NAPOLEON III
1861-1871

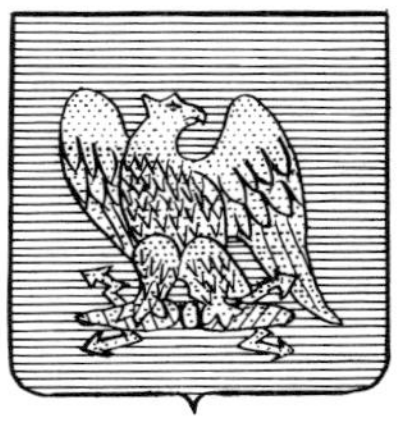

SUCHET D'ALBUFERA
1895-1896

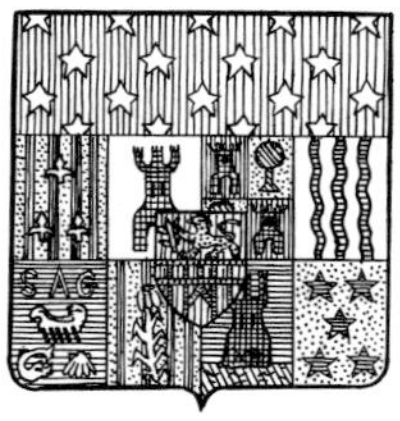

On September 6th, 1870, a decree of the provisional Government allotted Malmaison to the State. During the siege of Paris, it was the scene of violent fighting on October 21st, then on January 19th, 1871. Traces can still be seen on the drawing-room fireplace. In 1877, the Louvre Museum took back the statues in the park that had once been lent to Josephine; on November 6th the domain, now reduced to 43 hectares, was sold for 731,000 F, then parcelled out. The château, surrounded by 6 hectares of garden, passed from hand to hand till the financier Daniel Osiris-Iffla, better known under the name of Osiris, bought it for 132,000 F on August 12th, 1896, restored it at great expense and offered it to the State on December 14th 1903, on the condition that a Napoleonic museum should be created there and the furniture and objects that had decorated it during the Consulate, be replaced as far as possible. The donation was accepted on January 25th, 1904, while the museum was opened in 1906 and has been constantly enriched since then. The Empress Eugénie used to go there incognito at the end of her long life and made it generous gifts. Some important patrons, both French and foreign, held it an honour to complete the enterprise by donating the domaine of Bois-Préau and various fine napoleonic souvenirs.

Thus the wishes of the exile of Saint-Helena who had so loved his Malmaison, were partly fulfilled.

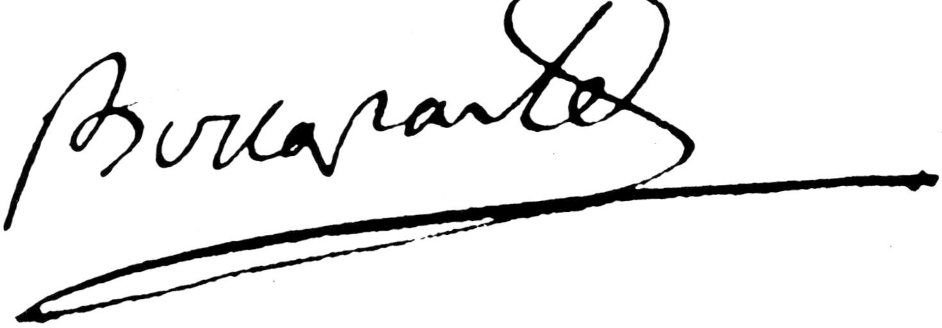

46
Jean-Baptiste Isabey. The First Consul at Malmaison, 1802. Drawing in black pencil and graphite, washed with chinese-ink and heightened with gouache on beige-coloured paper, signed. From Josephine's former collection at Malmaison.

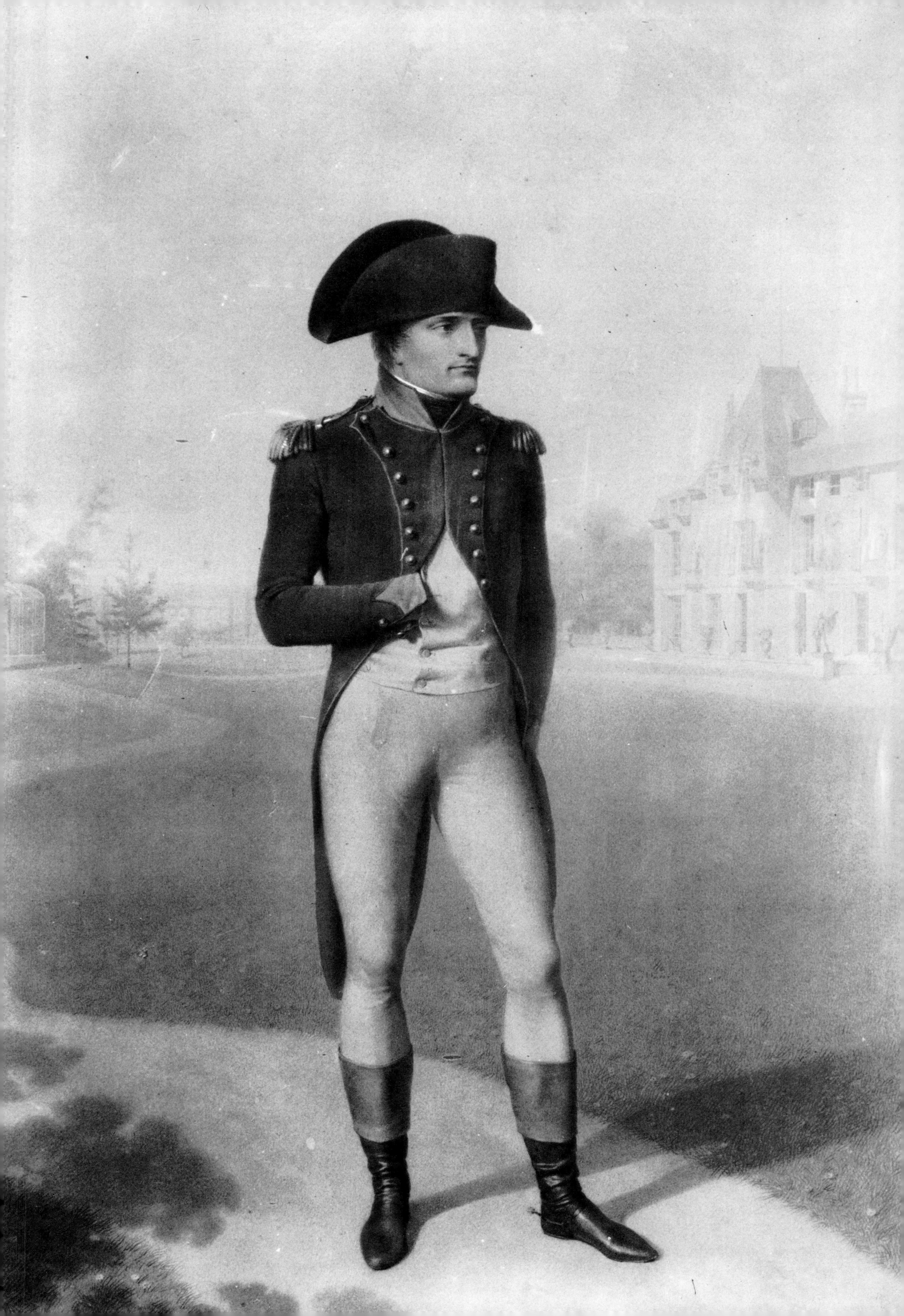

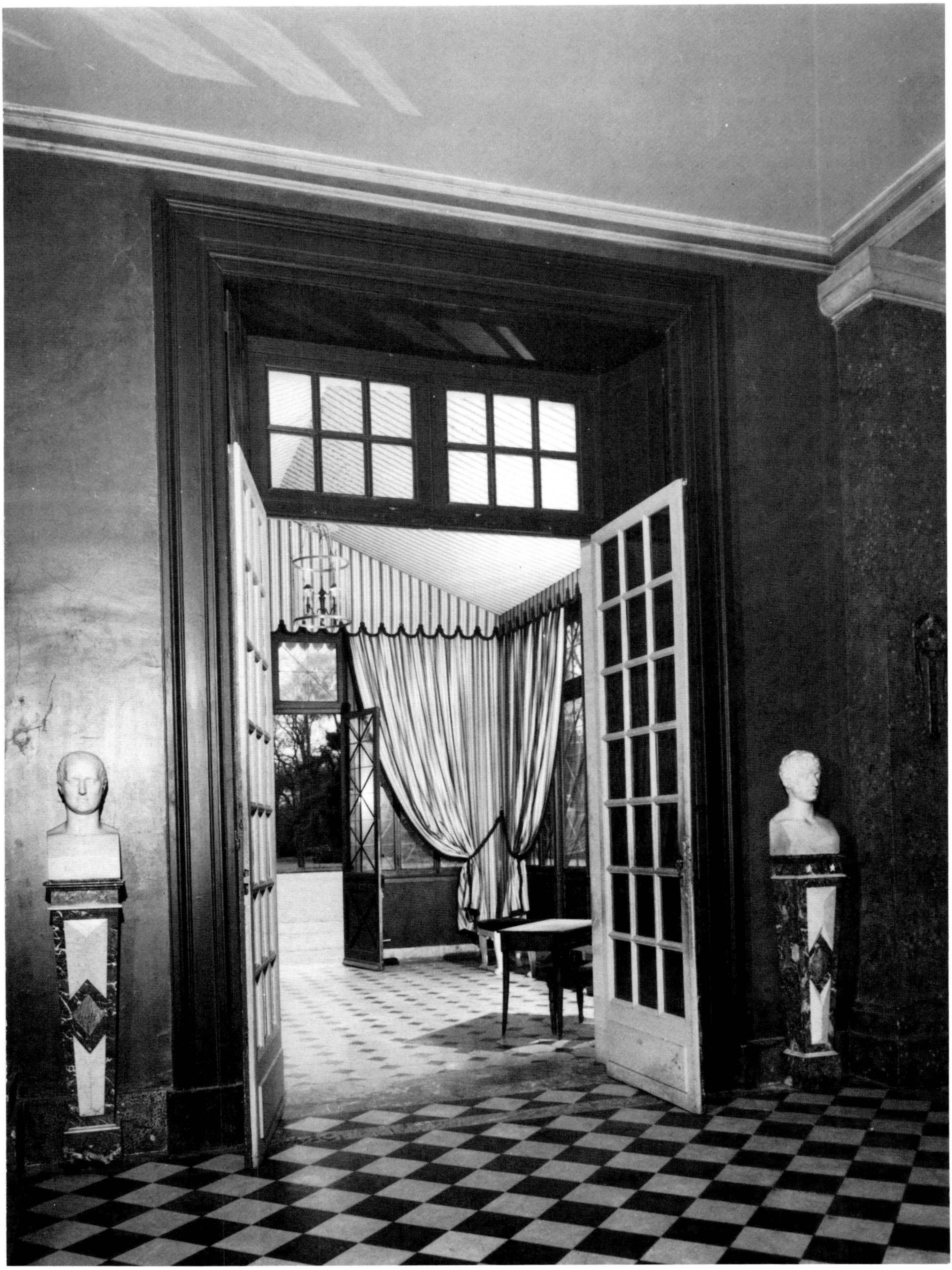

47
The verandah seen from the main hall, by Fontaine and Percier, 1800. Busts of Napoleon's brothers Joseph and Louis, Kings of Spain and Holland, in Carrara marble, on the left and right of the door, after Delaistre and Cartellier.

49
The château, façade on the main courtyard, seen from the main entrance.

48
The main hall. In the centre, a Carrara marble basin from Malmaison (gift of Grand-Duke Nicolas Mikailovitch, 1912). Bust of Madame Letizia Bonaparte, marble, after Dupaty; posthumous bust of Charles Bonaparte, marble, after Marin (gifs of Mme Raba Deutsch de la Meurthe, 1930) and bust of Napoleon after Chaudet.

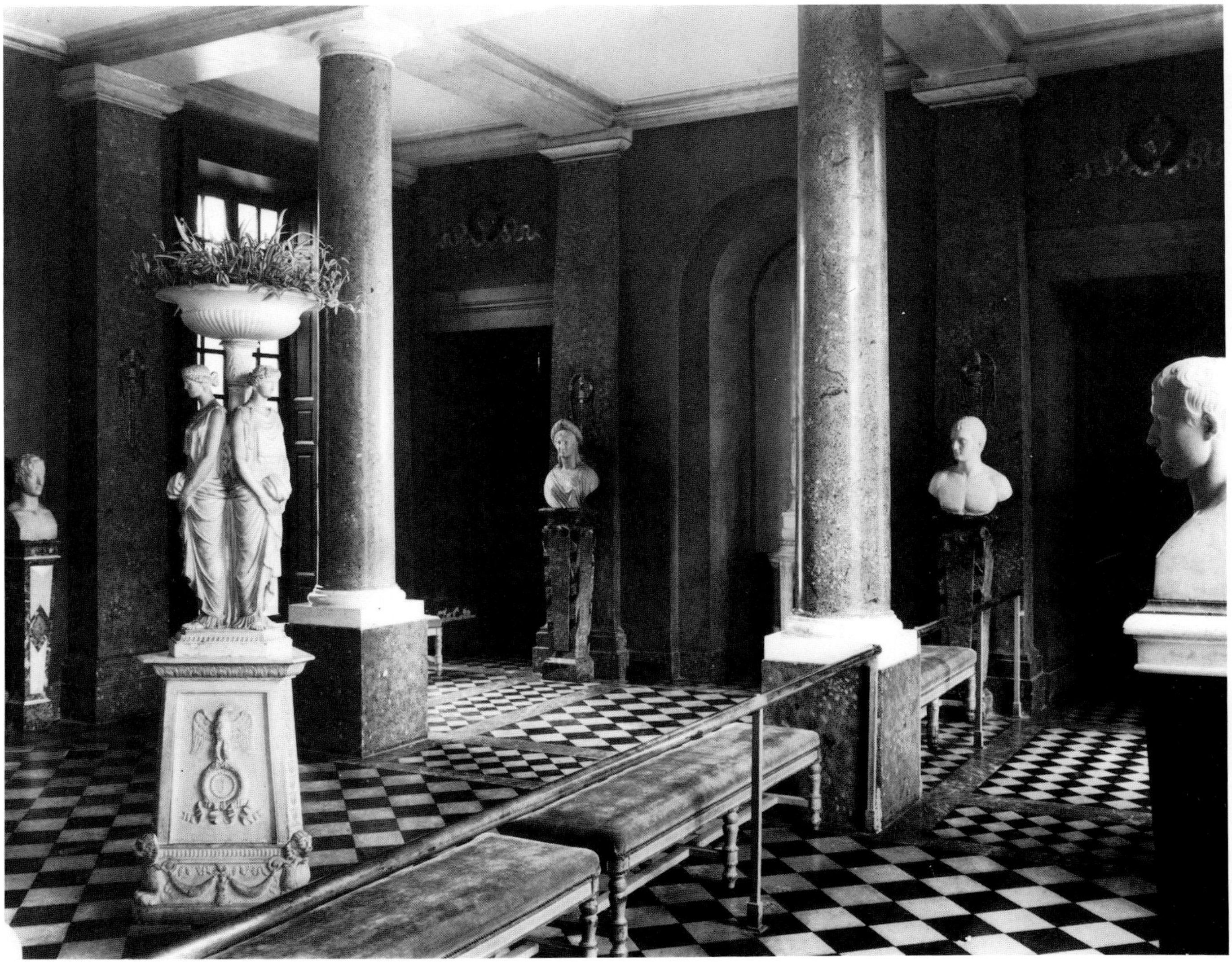

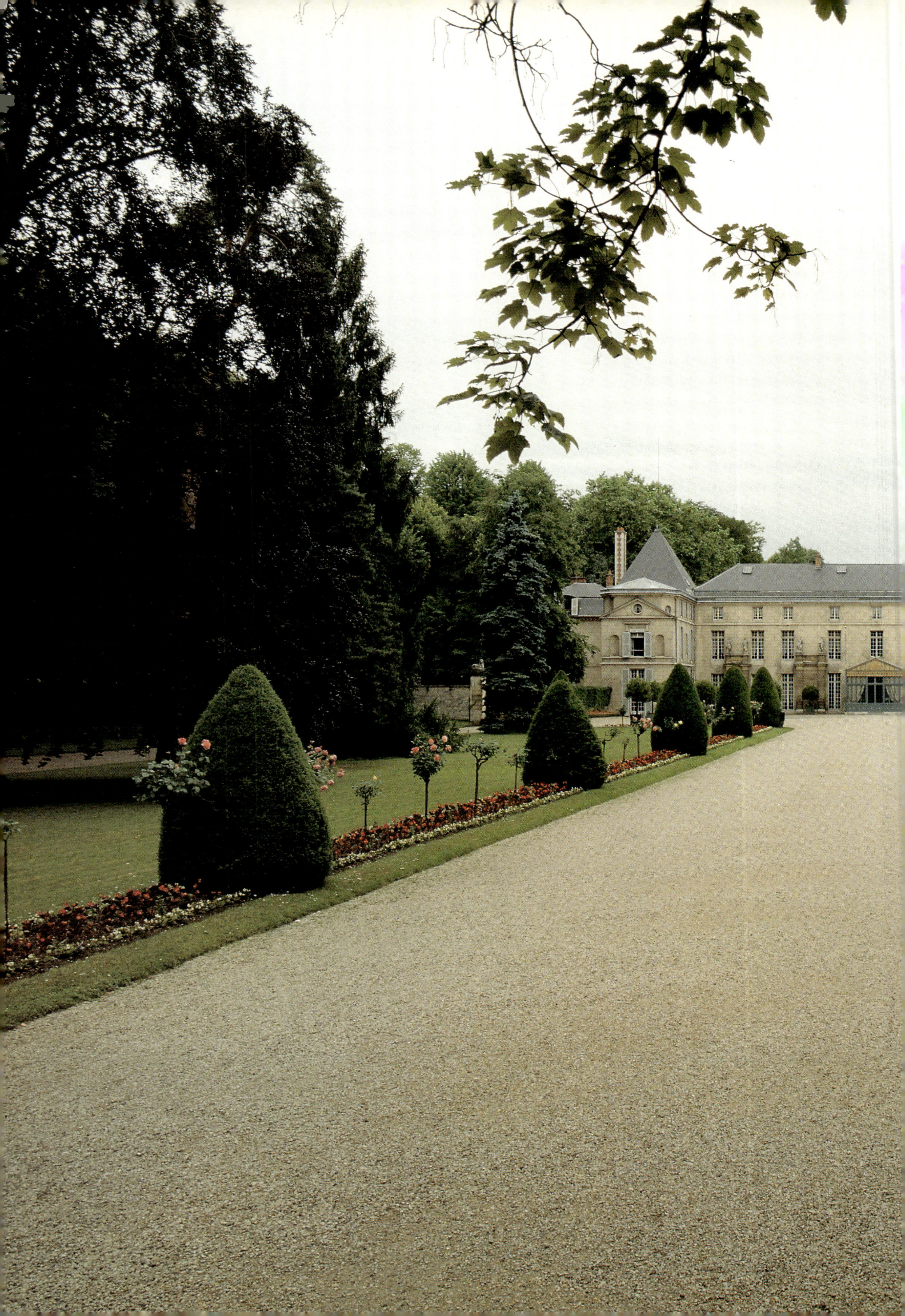

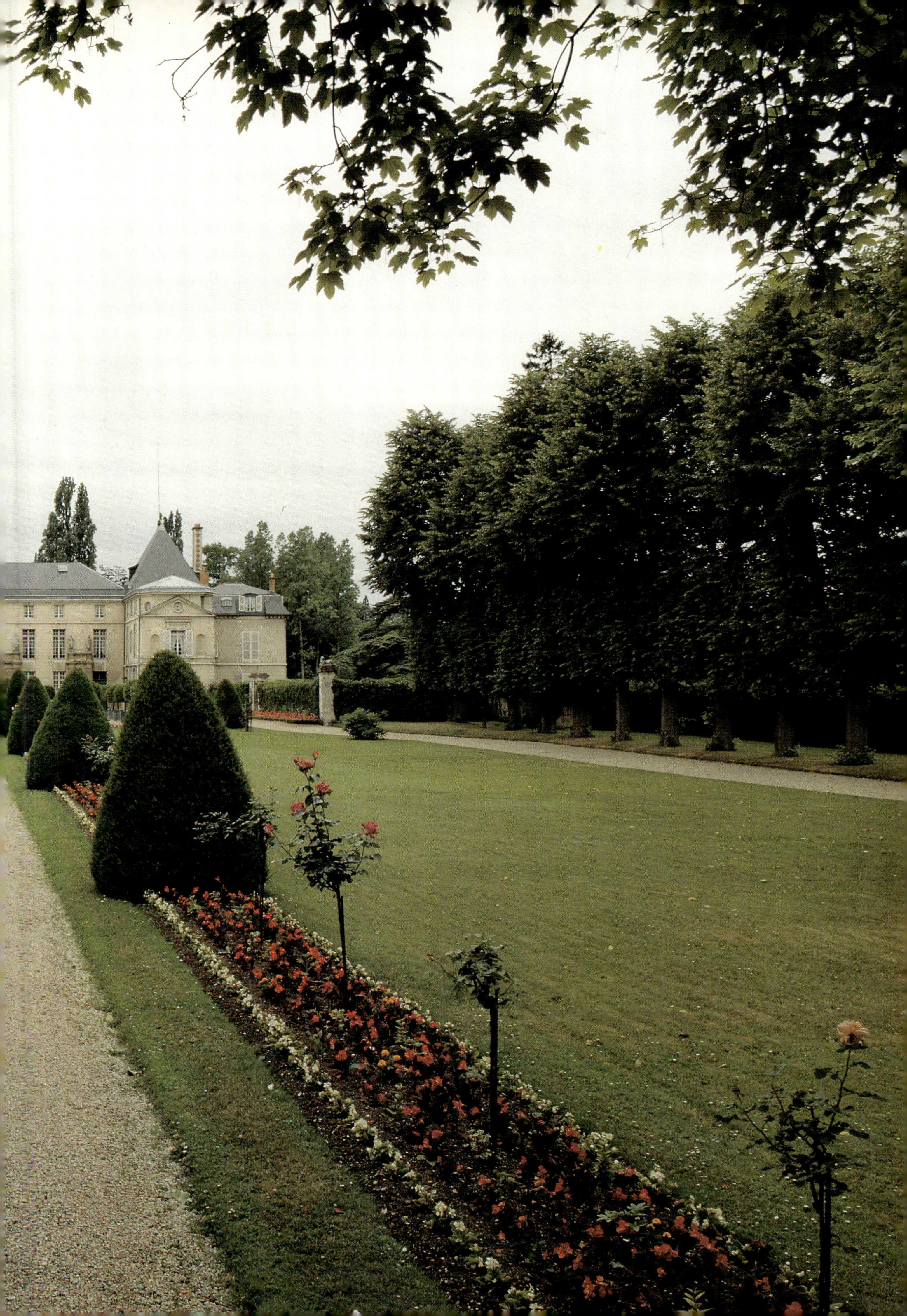

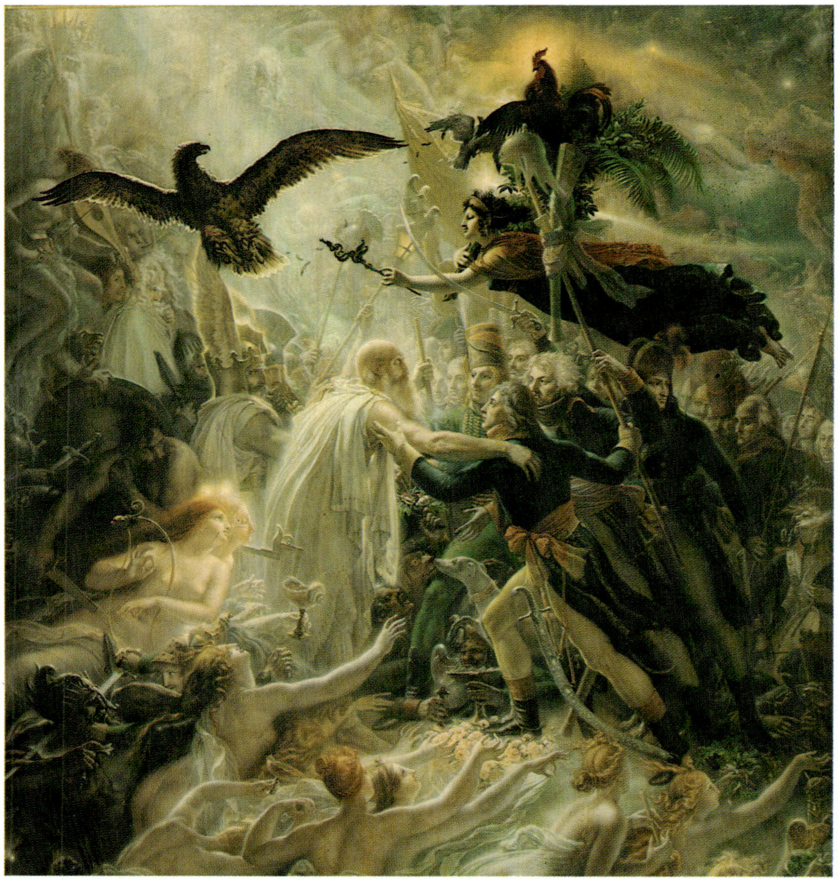

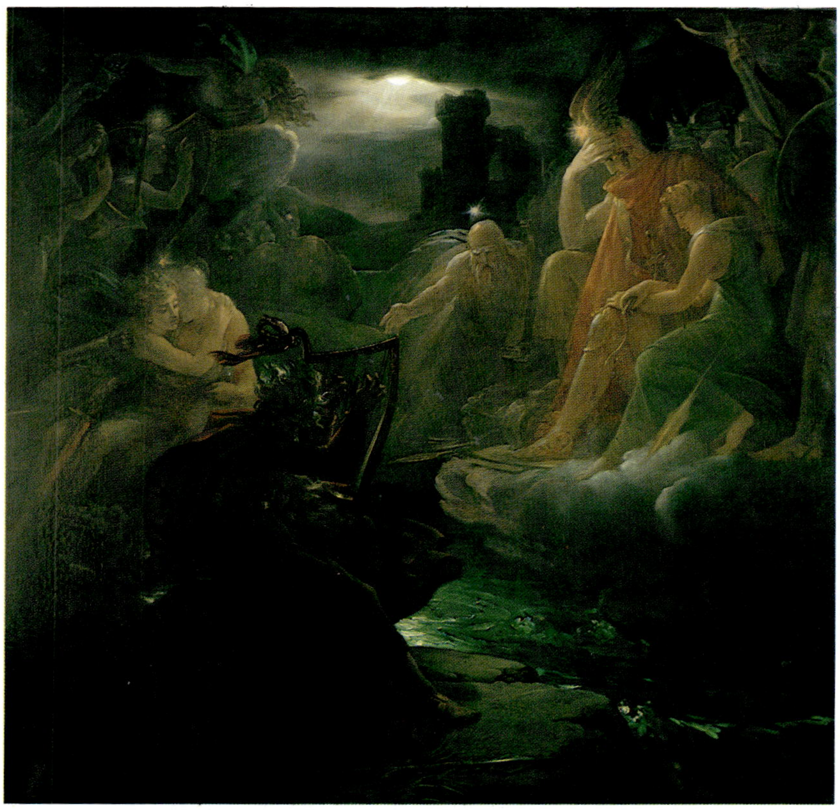

50
Anne-Louis Girodet-Trioson (1767-1824). The apotheosis of the French heroes who died for their country during the war of liberation. The bard Ossian welcomes to the Paradise of the brave the shades of Frenchmen, among whom we recognize Hoche, Marceau, Desaix, Kléber... Painting commissioned for this place, 1801-1802.

51
François Gérard (1770-1837). Ossian calls up the shades to the sound of his harp on the banks of the Lora. An old replica of the painting commissioned for this place in 1800 and inspired by the Caledonian poems much appreciated by Napoleon.

52
The small drawing-room: marble fireplace offered by the Pope, portrait of Queen Hortense by Girodet (left), seats from Saint-Cloud.

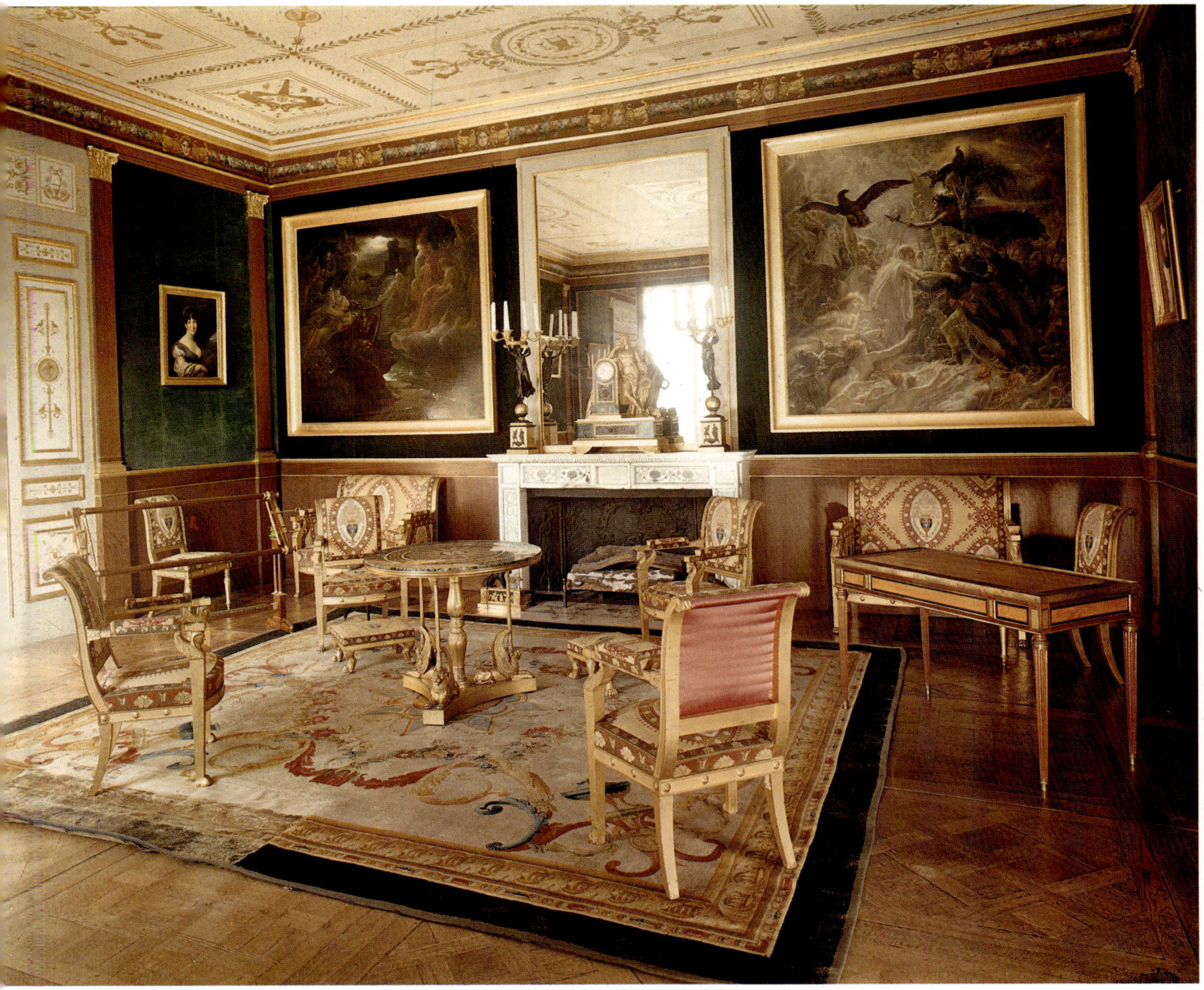

53
Auguste Garneray (1785-1824). The music-room in 1812, signed water-colour (gift of Empress Eugénie). The room was at that time prolonged by the Great Gallery, since demolished. Bergeret's painting "Tribute paid to Raphael after his death" is back in its place (right).

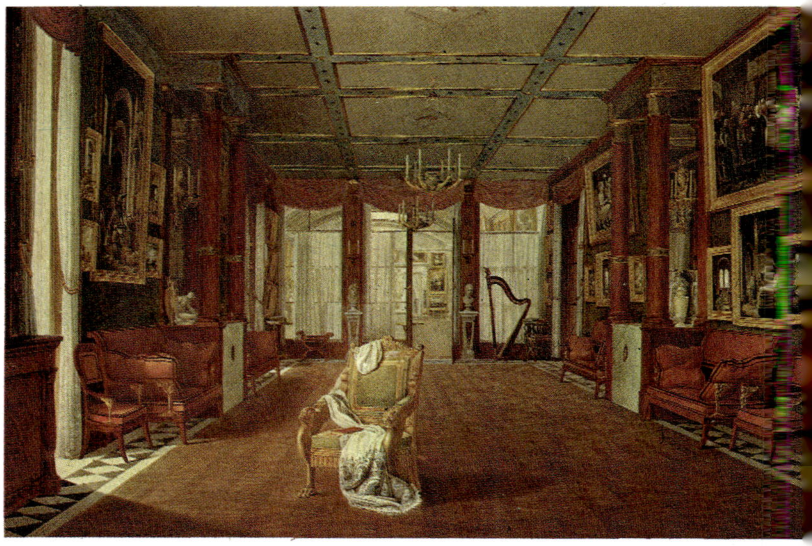

54
Music-room. The harp by Cousineau and the Jacob brothers' sofas and armchairs are in place.

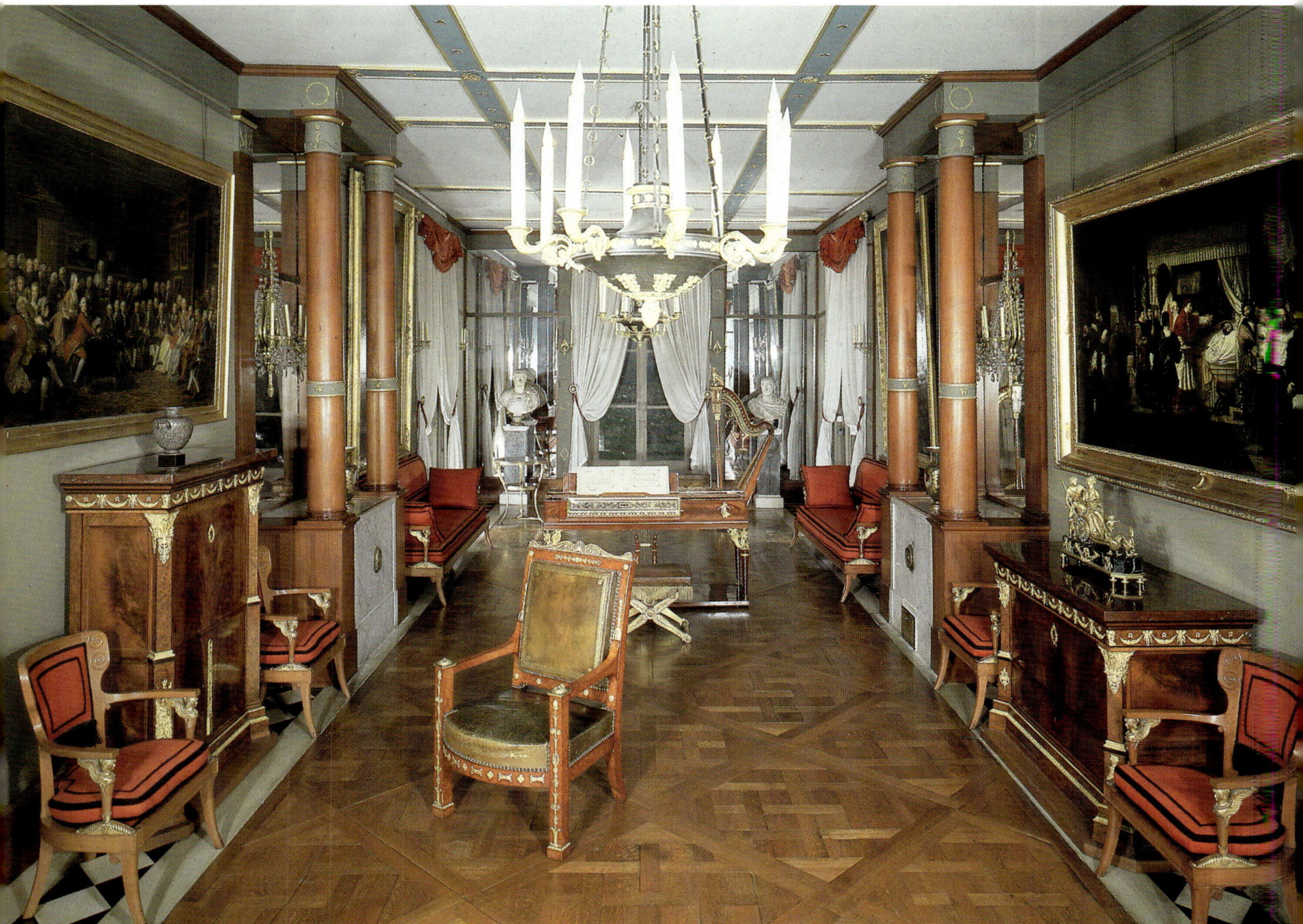

55
The dining-room, arranged by Fontaine and Percier in 1800 with alterations by Berthault in 1812.

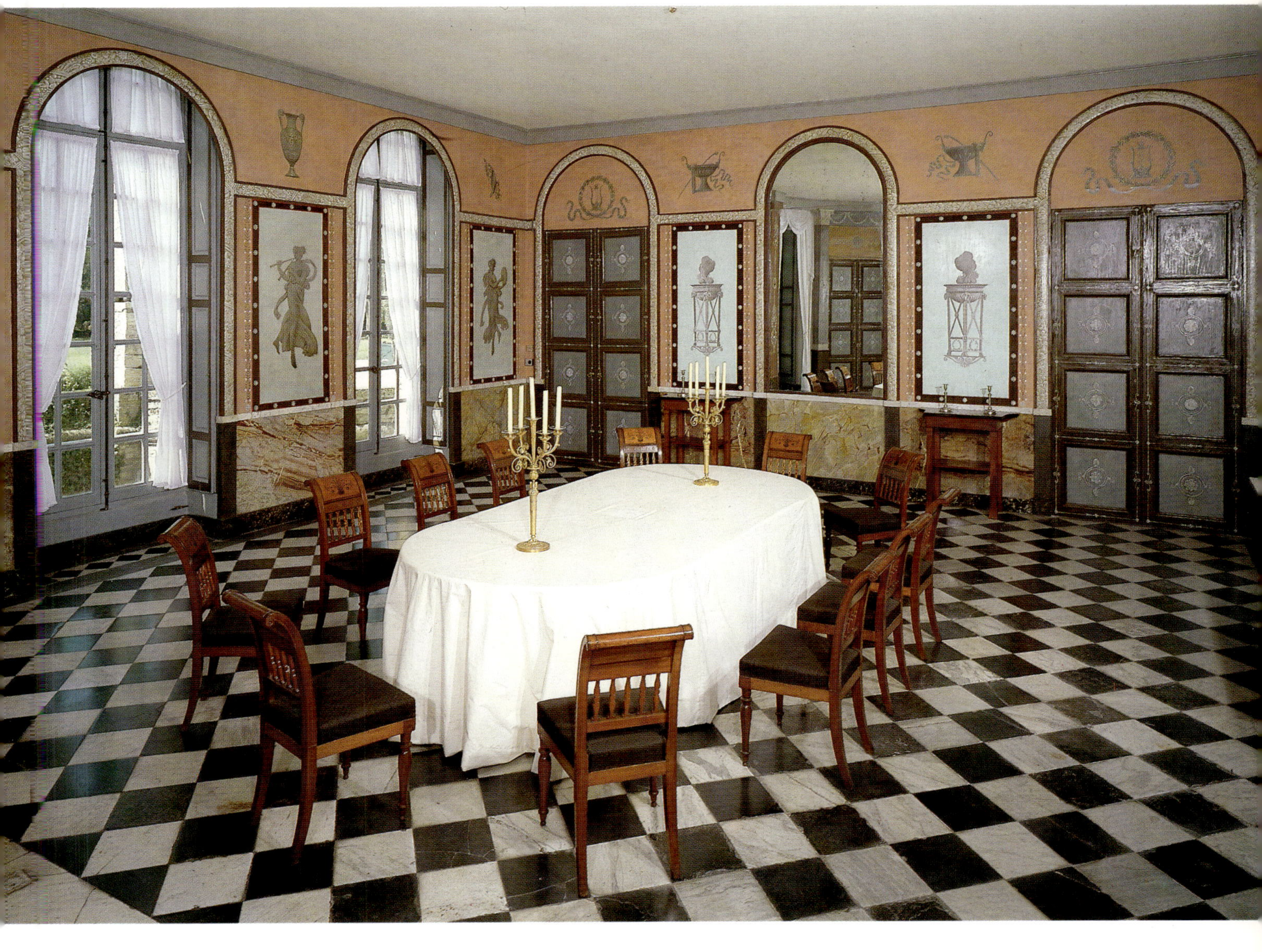

56
Statuette of Minerva in the shape of a clock. Patinated and gilded bronze. By Galle (gift Cates, 1939).

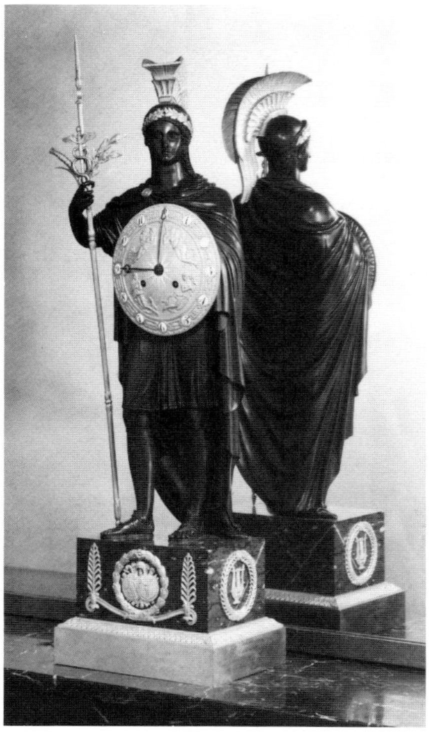

5
The Council Chambe
fitted up in 1800 by Fonta
and Percier. The stools by the Jac
brothers are back in their pla

57
The Council Chamber. Engraving from "Recueil de Décorations intérieures" by Percier and Fontaine.

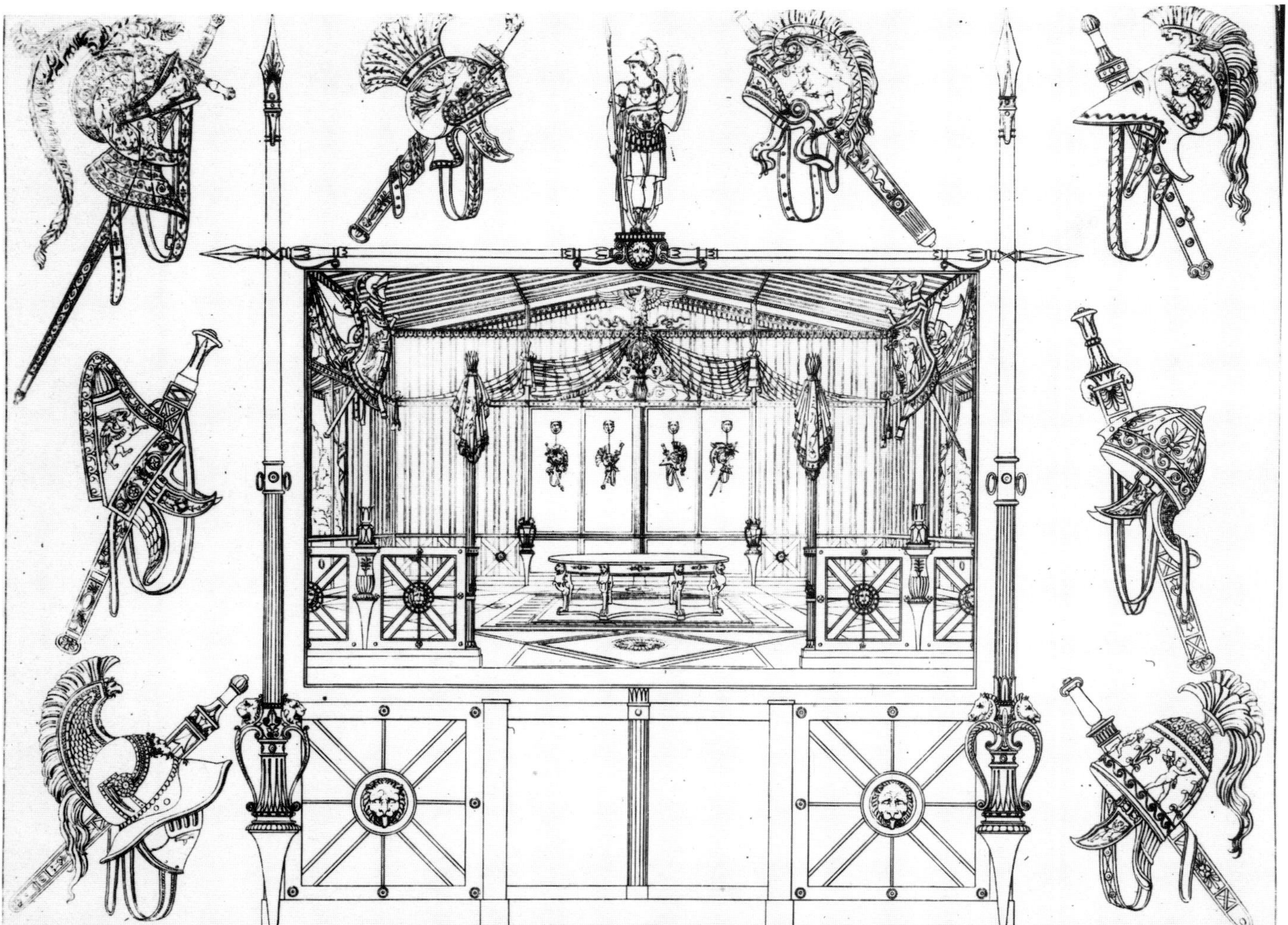

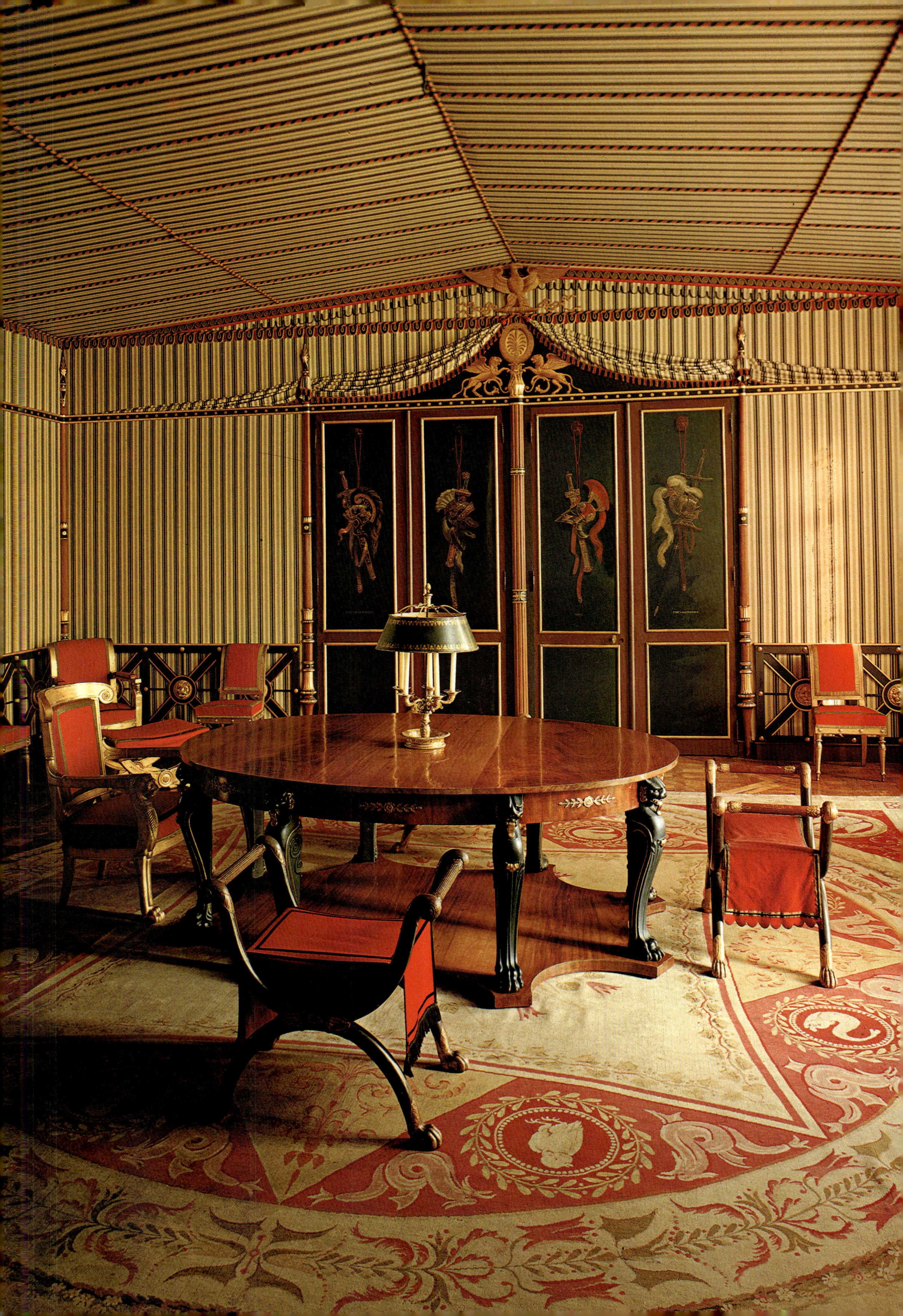

59
Detail of the ceiling of the library. Engraving from "Recueil de Décorations intérieures" by Percier and Fontaine.

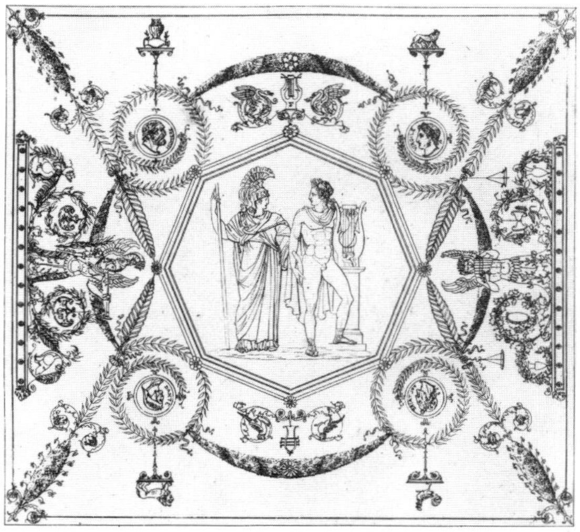

61
The library decorated in 1800 by Percier and Fontaine with the collaboration of the Jacob brothers and of Moench

60
The library.
Engraving from the same volume.

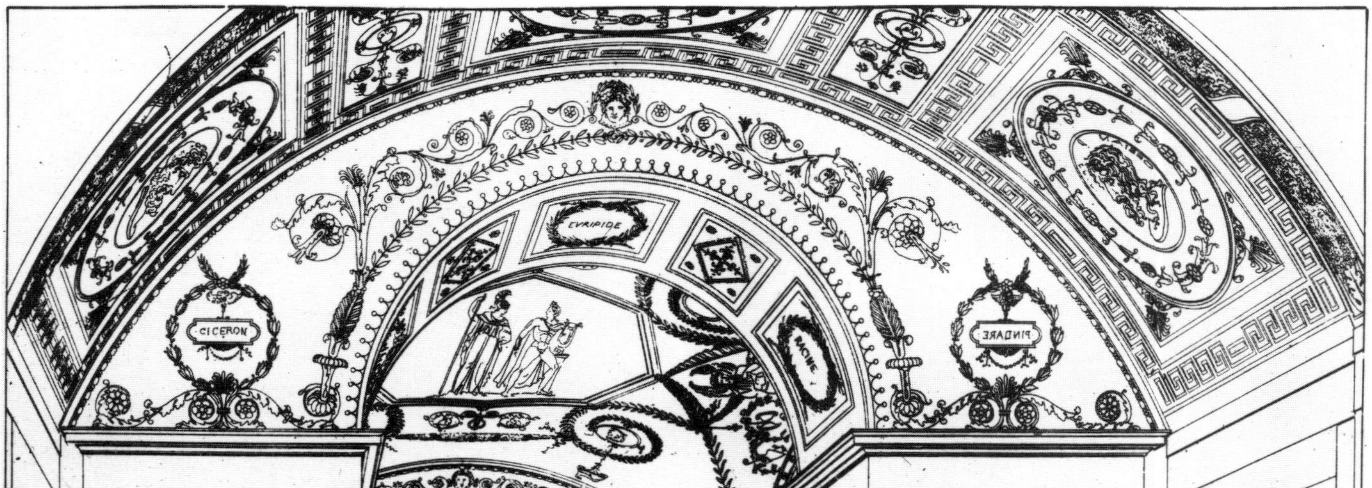

Ch. Percier et Fontaine.

Vue perspective de la Bibliotheque éxécutée à la M.on

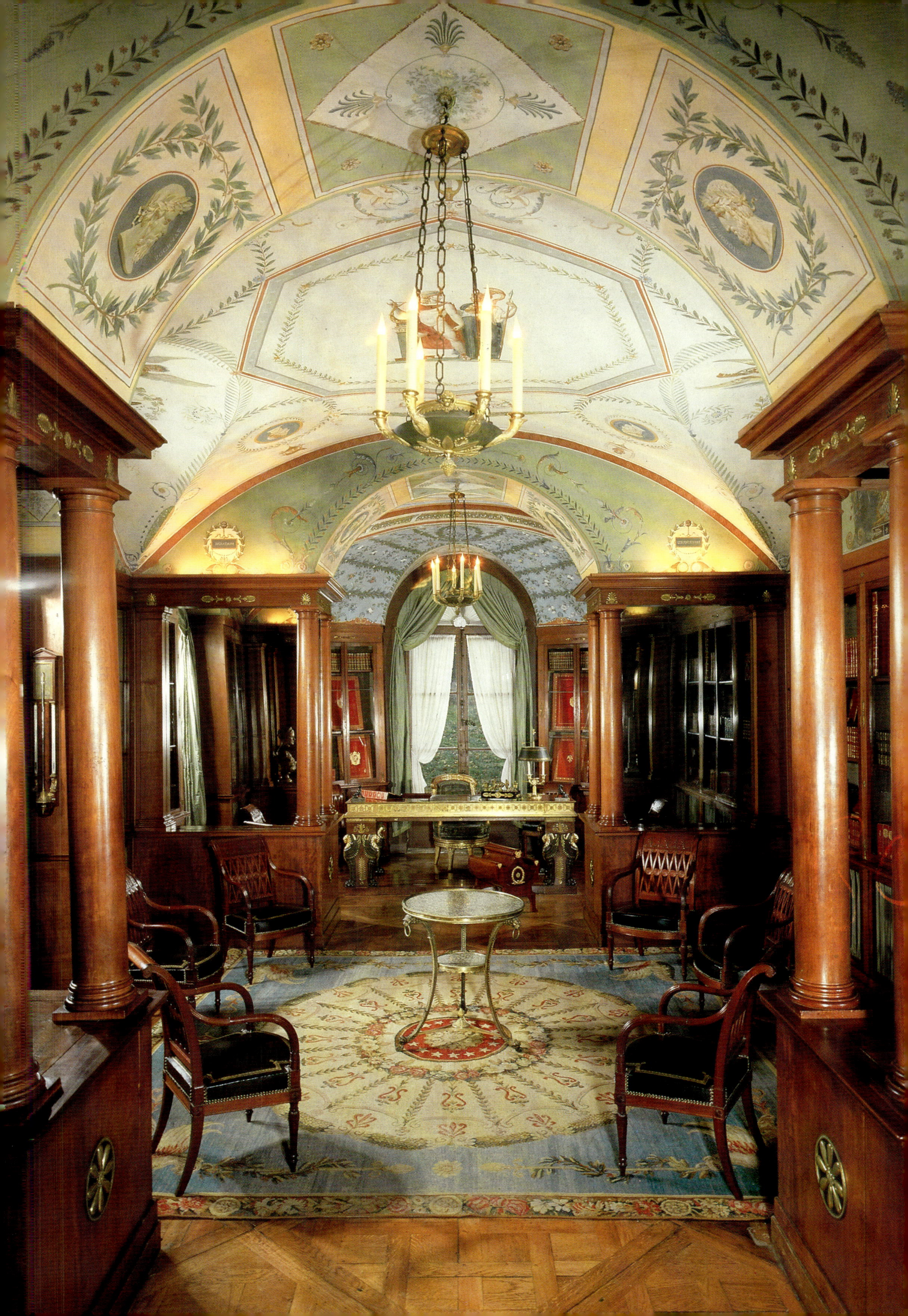

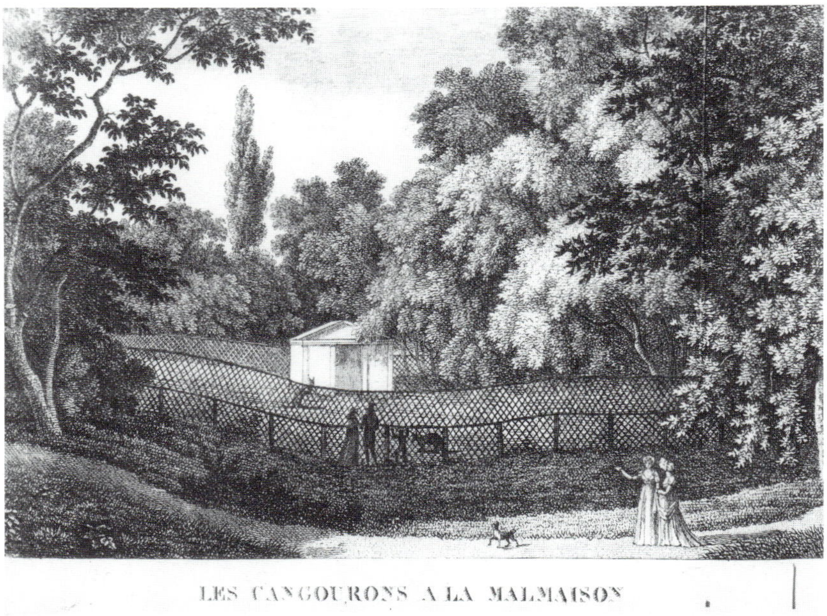

62
The kangaroos at Malmaison. Engraving.

63
Auguste Garneray. Promenade of the ladies-in-waiting by the river. Water-colour. Collection of the Empress (gift of D. David-Weill, 1935).

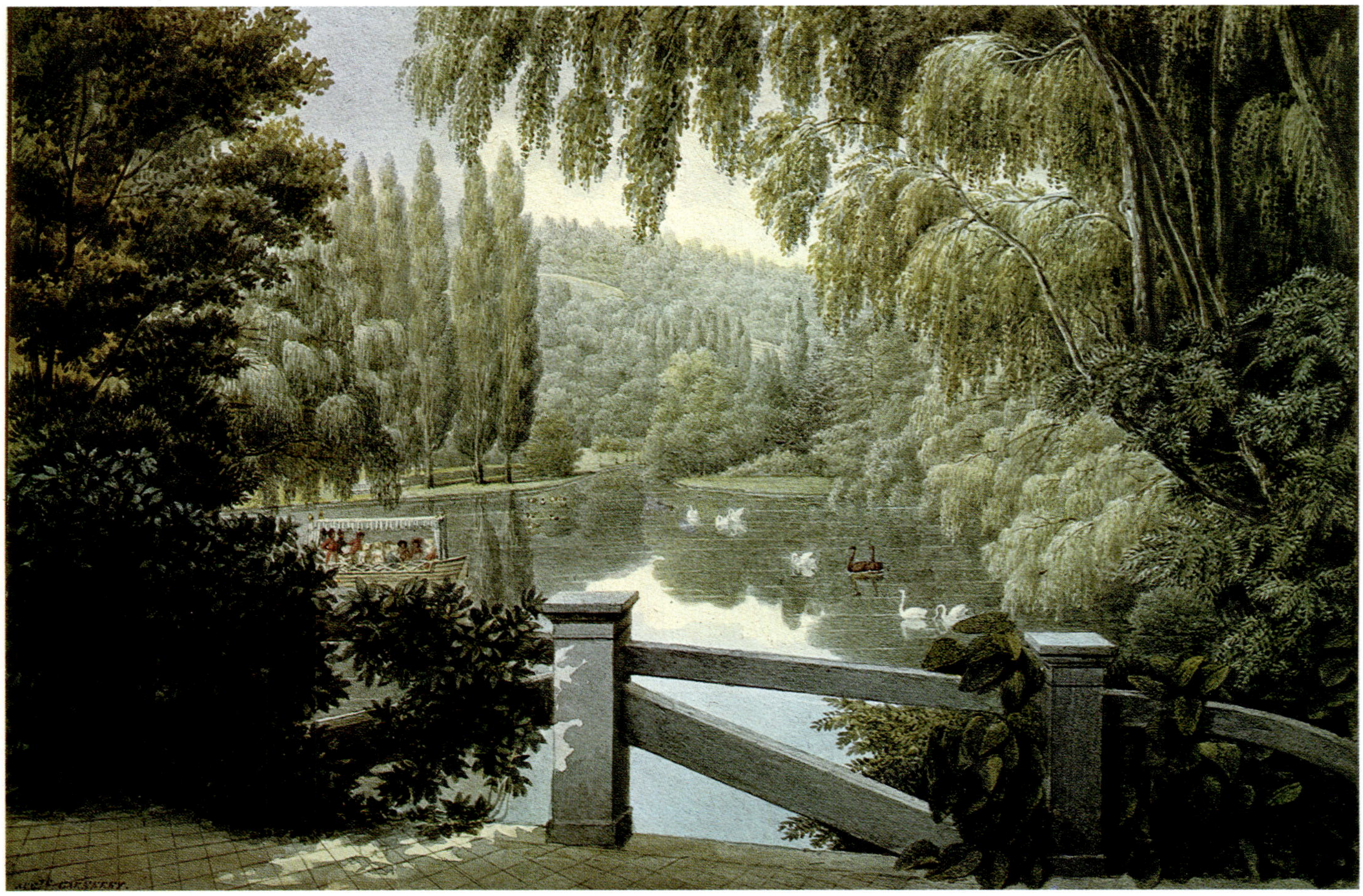

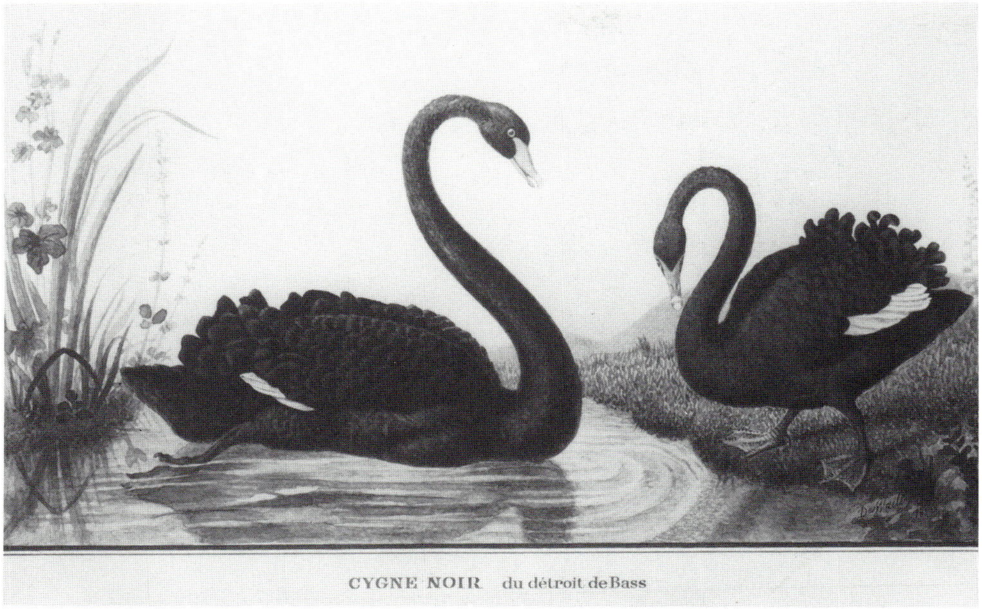

64
Black swans from the Bass Detroit, copy of the water-colour signed "de Wailly 1806", kept in the Natural History Museum of Paris.

65
Auguste Garneray. The Temple of Love on the river bank, with rhododendrons. Water-colour (gift D. David-Weill, 1935).

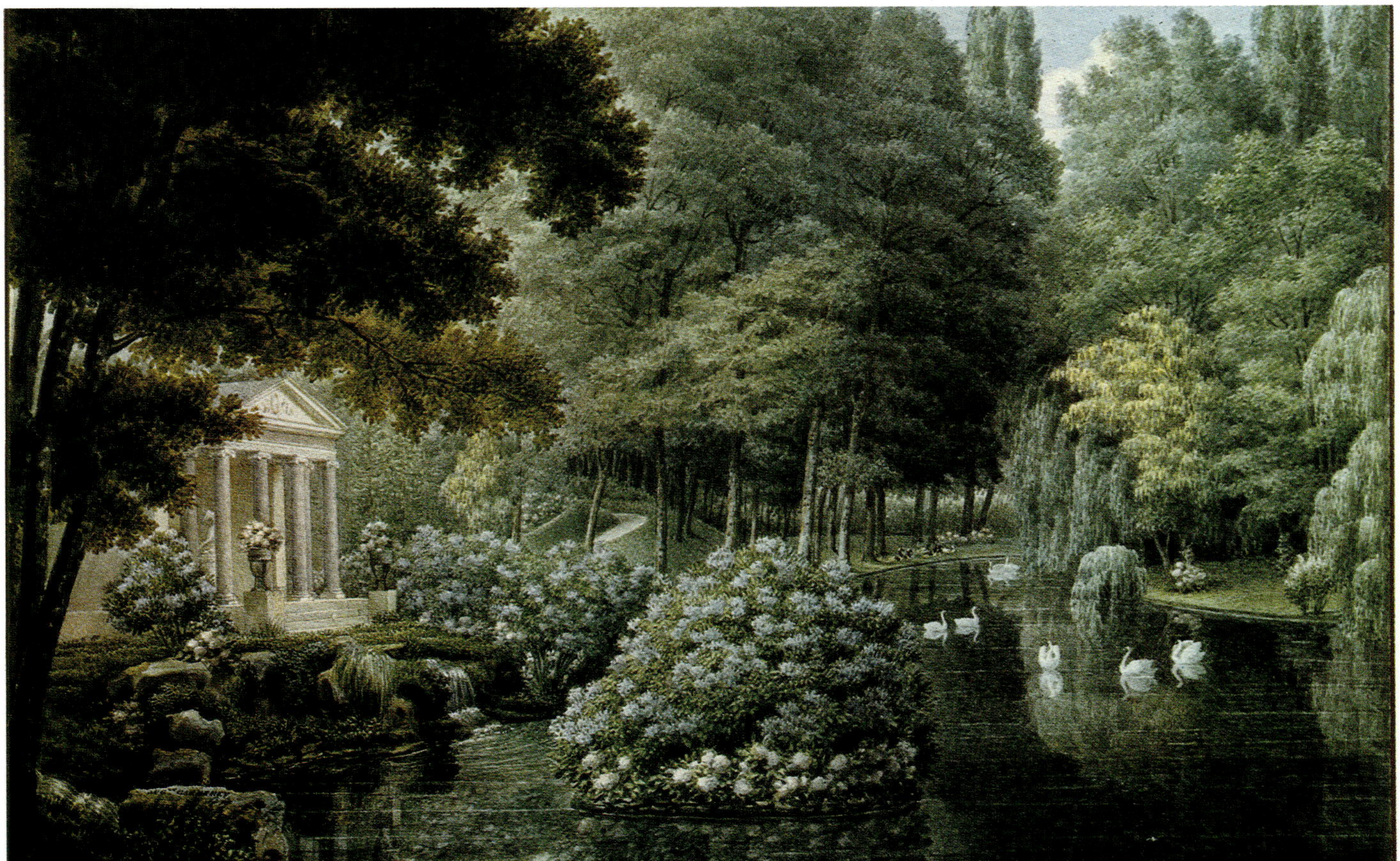

66
A view of the park. Modern rose-bed.

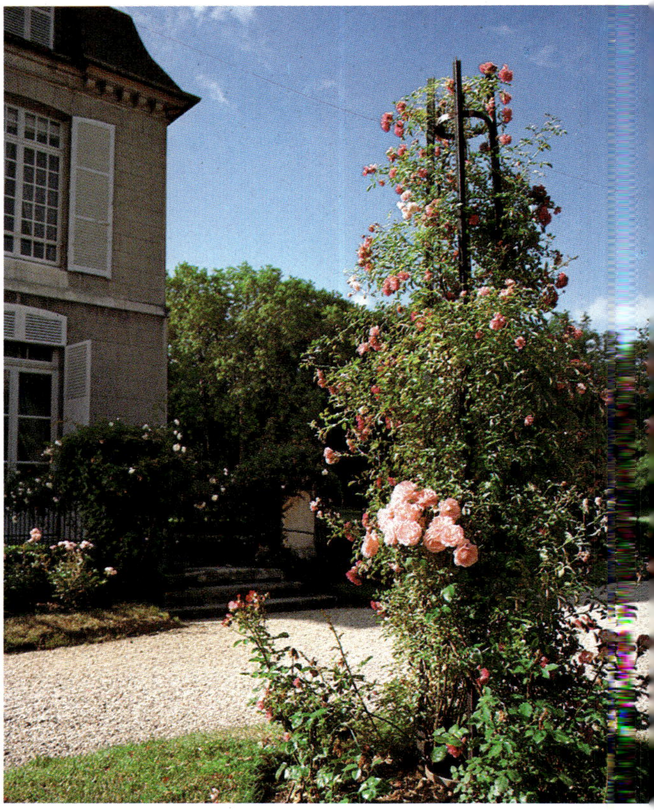

67
The château, West façade on the park, photograph taken from the "Marengo cedar".

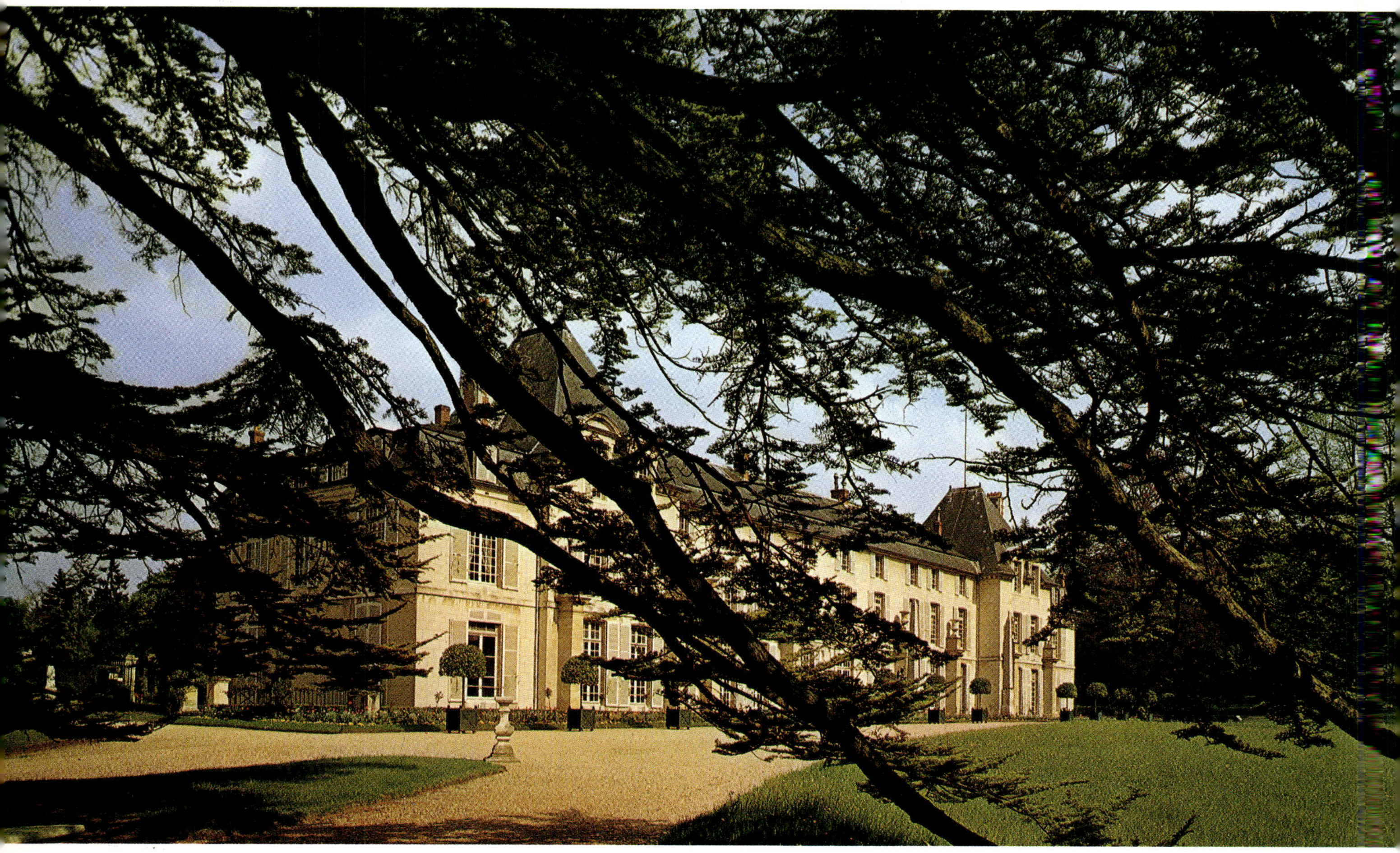

68
The South Pavilion: library windows overlooking the park.

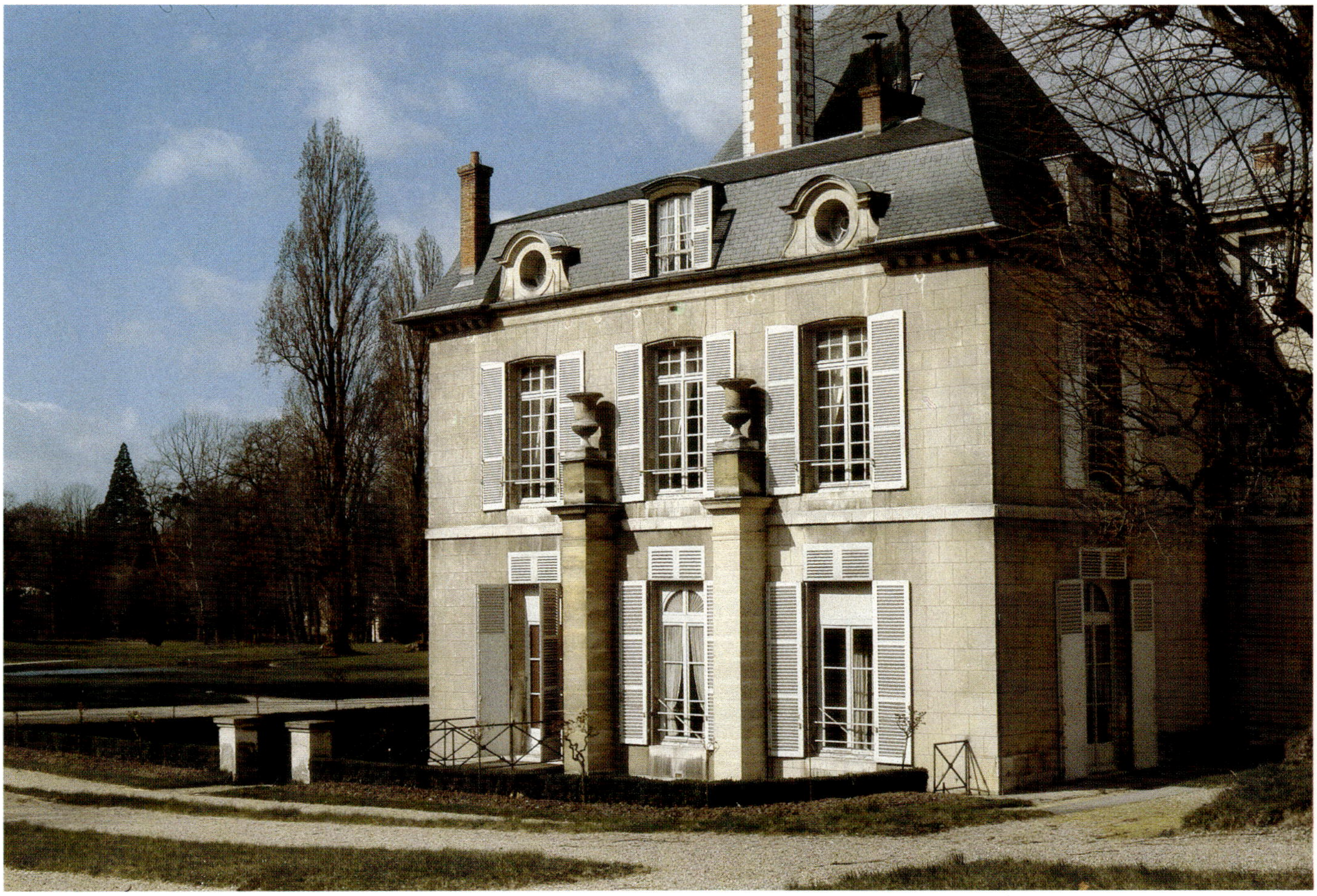

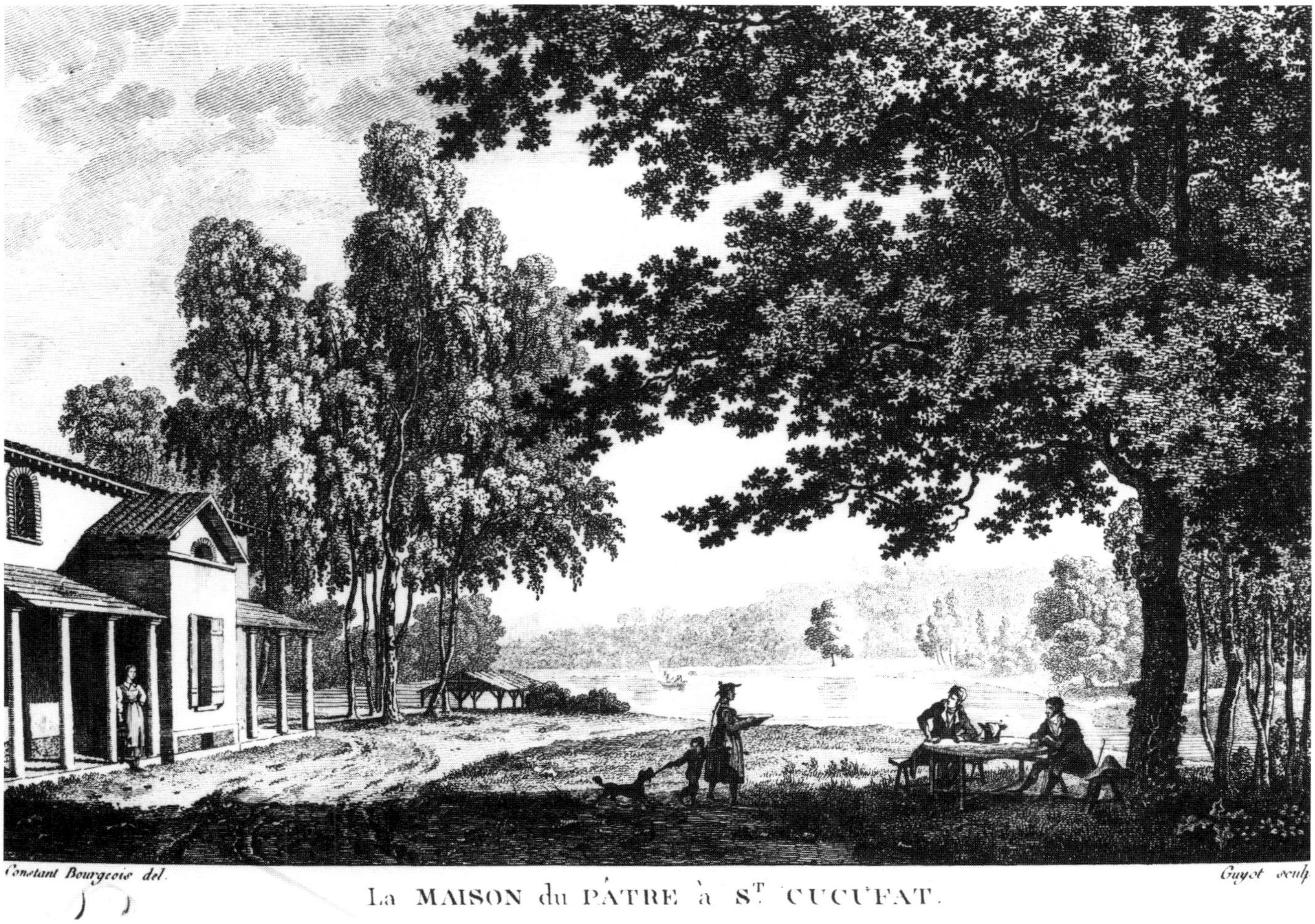

69
The "Cowherd's House" at Saint-Cucufat. Engraving by Guyot after Constant Bourgeois.

70
The Dairy. Black wash by Jean-Joseph Delorme (1815-1884).

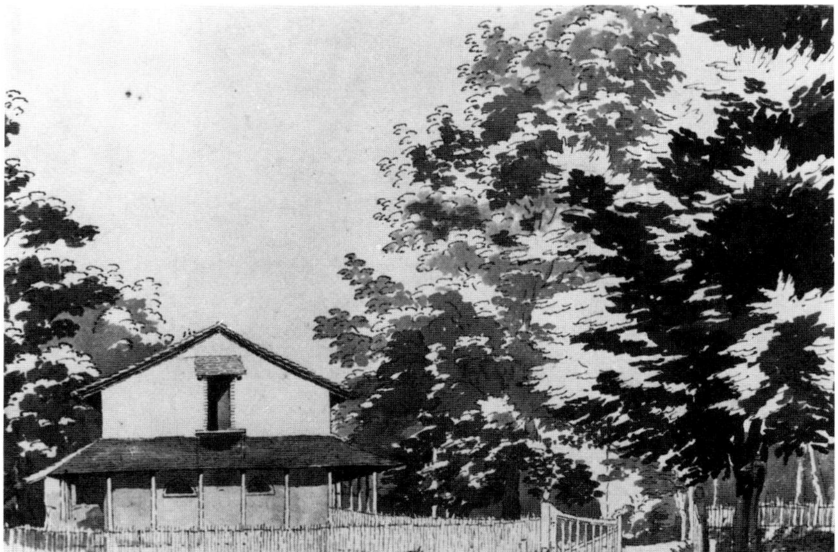

71
Auguste Garneray.
Visit to the hot-house.
Water-colour
(gift D. David-Weill, 1935).

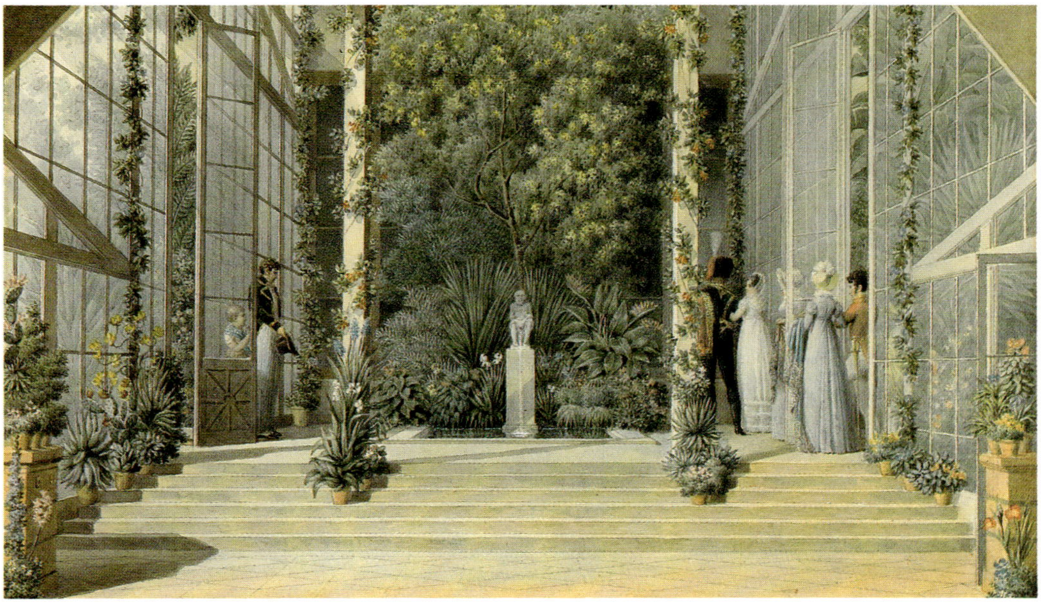

72
Auguste Garneray.
View of the hot-house.
Water-colour
(gift D. David-Weill, 1935).

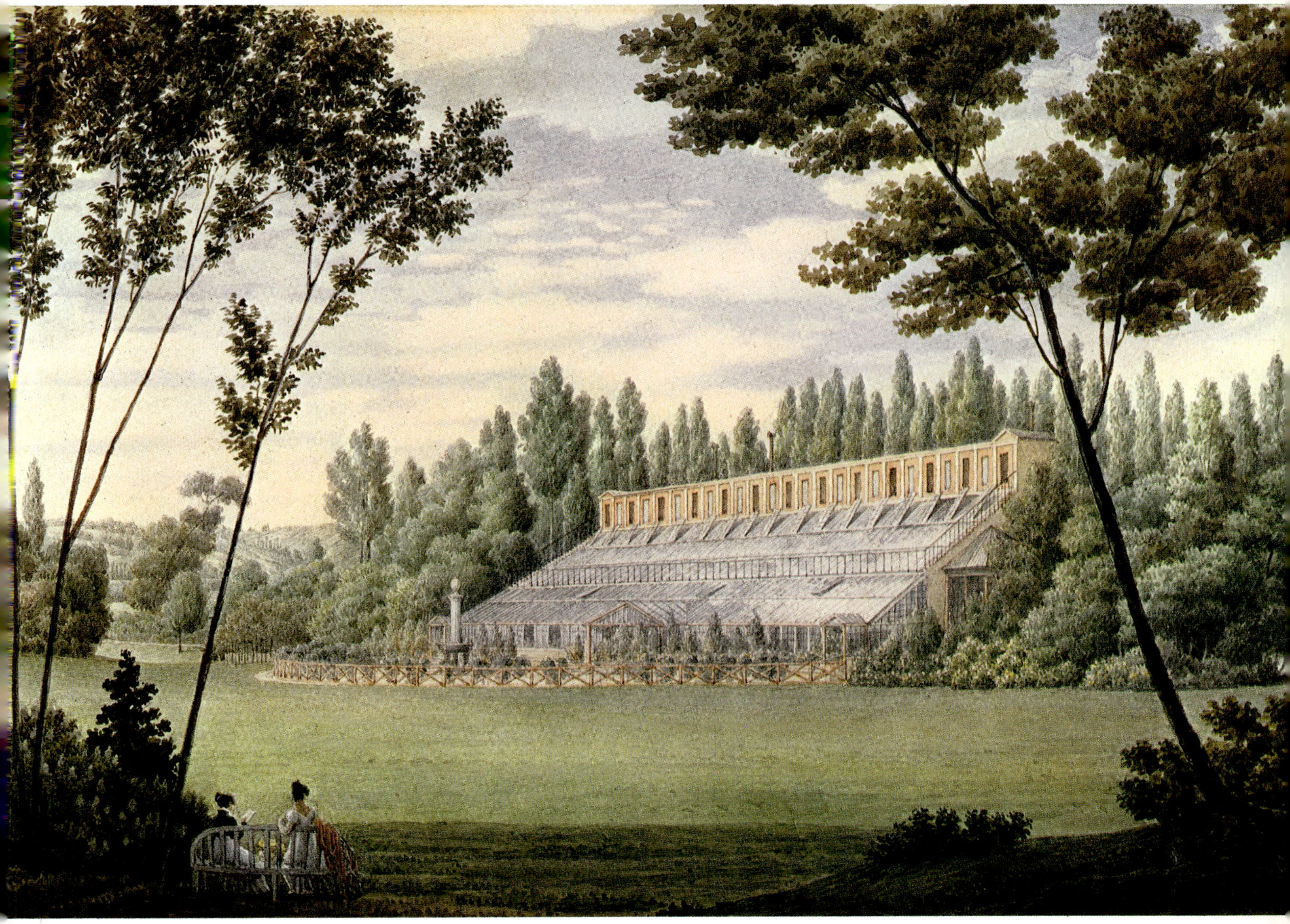

73
Love-rose, coloured engraving, taken from Roses, *drawn by Pierre-Joseph Redouté (1759-1840) and described by A. Thorry, volume published 1817-1824.*

74
François Gérard. Madame Bonaparte in her drawing-room at Malmaison, 1800-1801
(gift Edward Tuck, 1928).

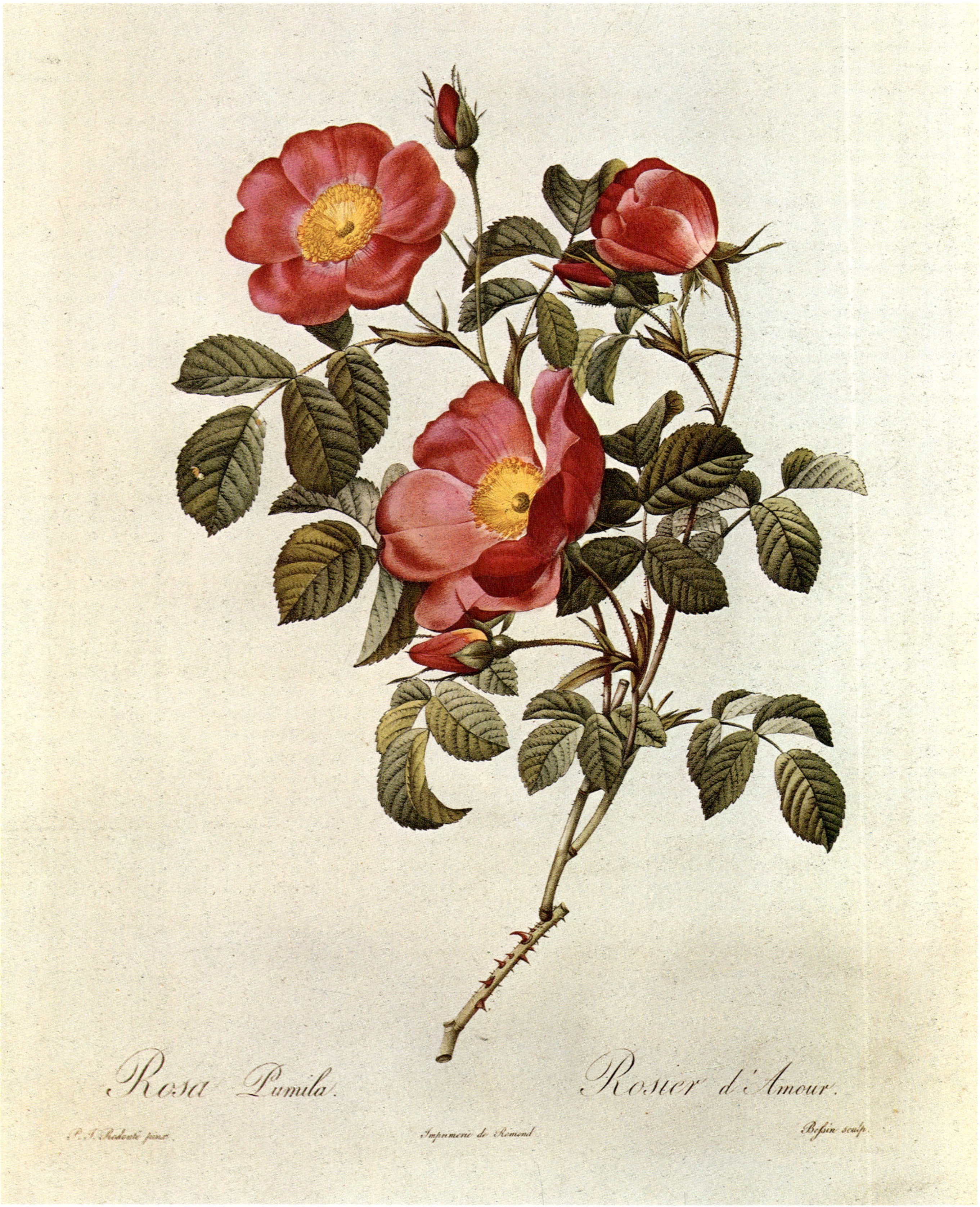

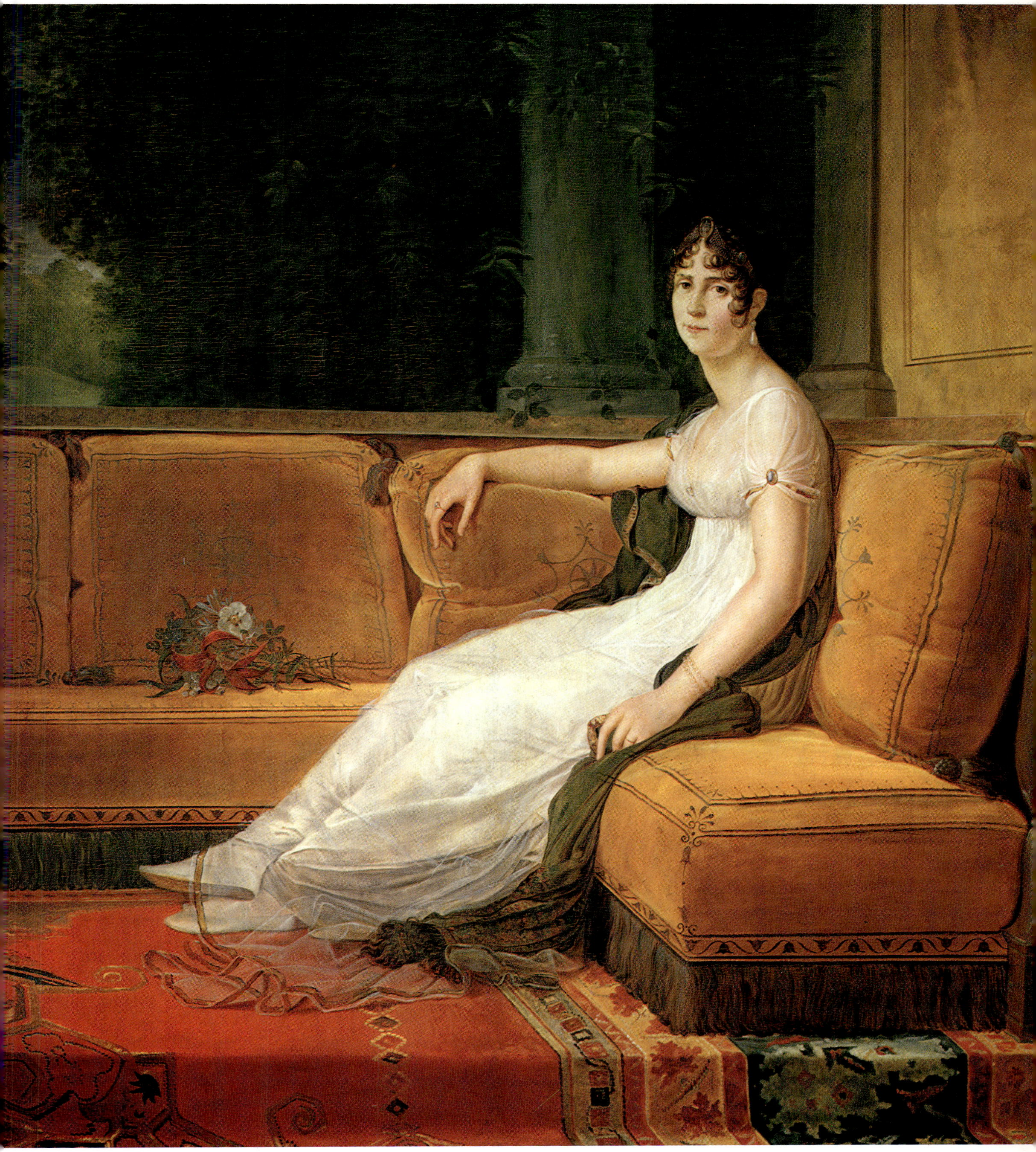

76
Antoine-Jean Gros (1771-1835). Empress Josephine, sketch for a full-length portrait now in the Masséna Museum in Nice, 1809.

75
Napoleon's bedchamber, restored according to the inventories with furniture from Les Tuileries and Saint-Cloud.

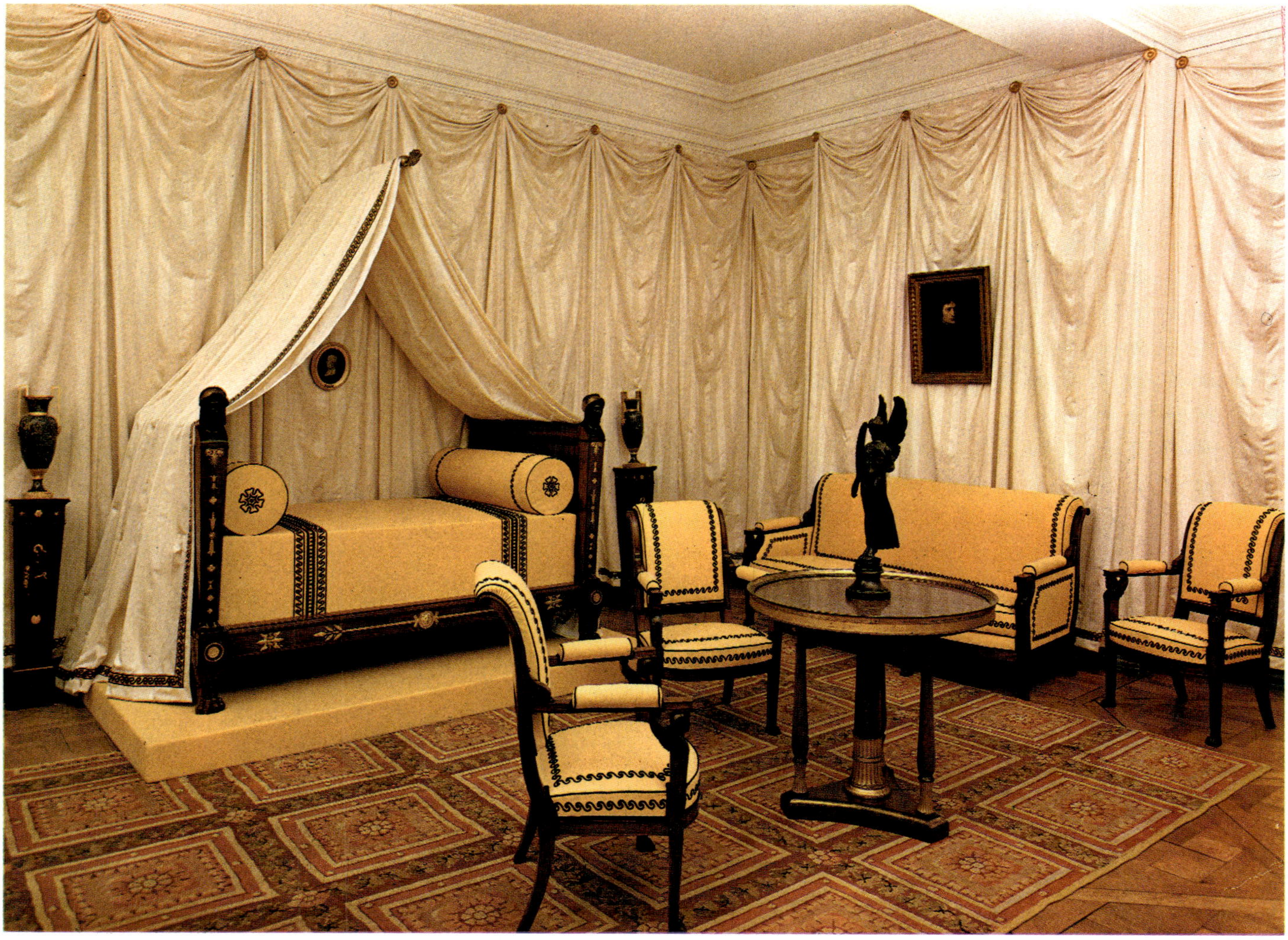

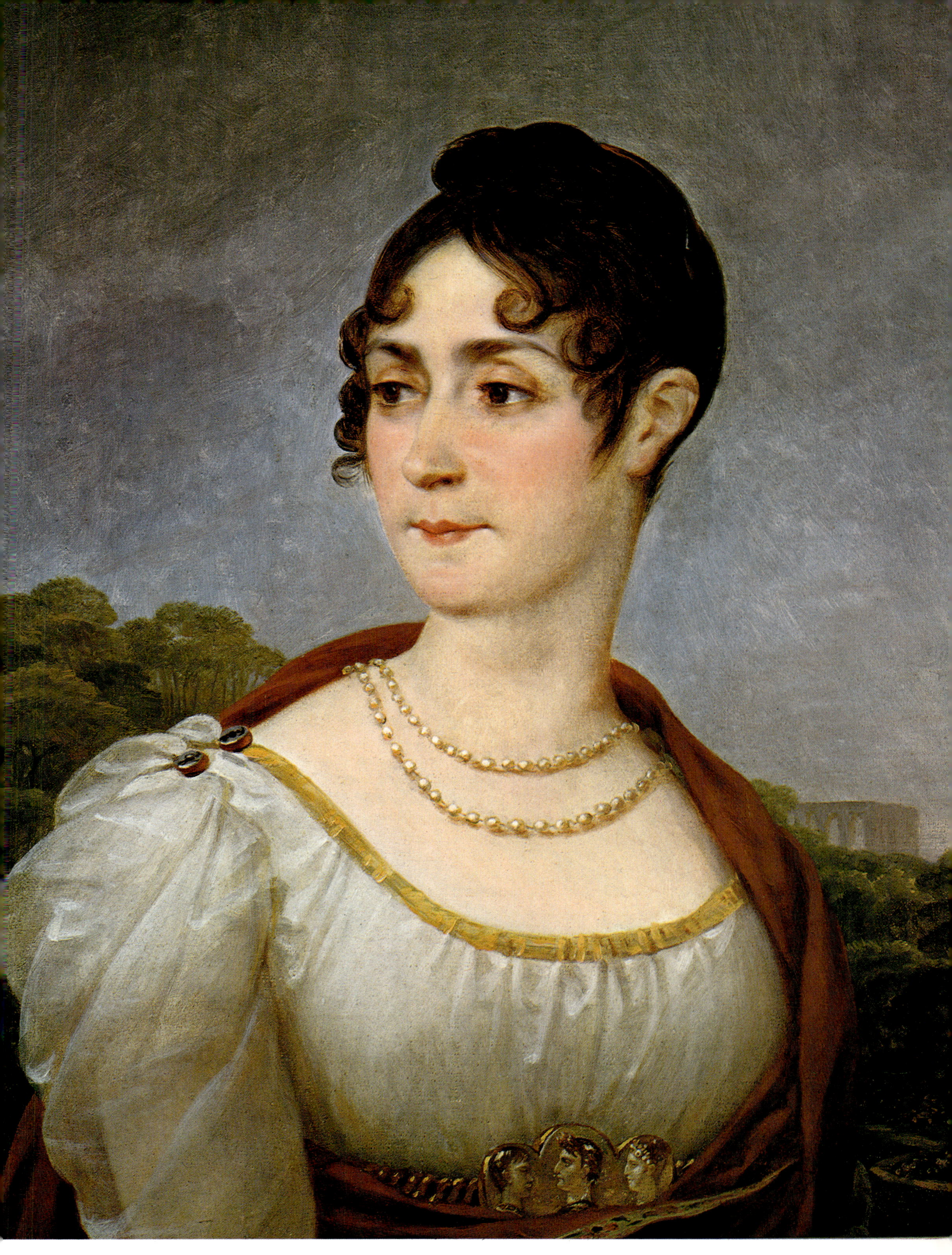

78
The Empress's bed, carved and gilded wood, signed Jacob-Desmalter, delivered short after 1812 when the bedchamber was refurnished.

77
Empress Josephine's court robe and mantle (or train). White tulle embroidered with a network of gold threads on white satin.

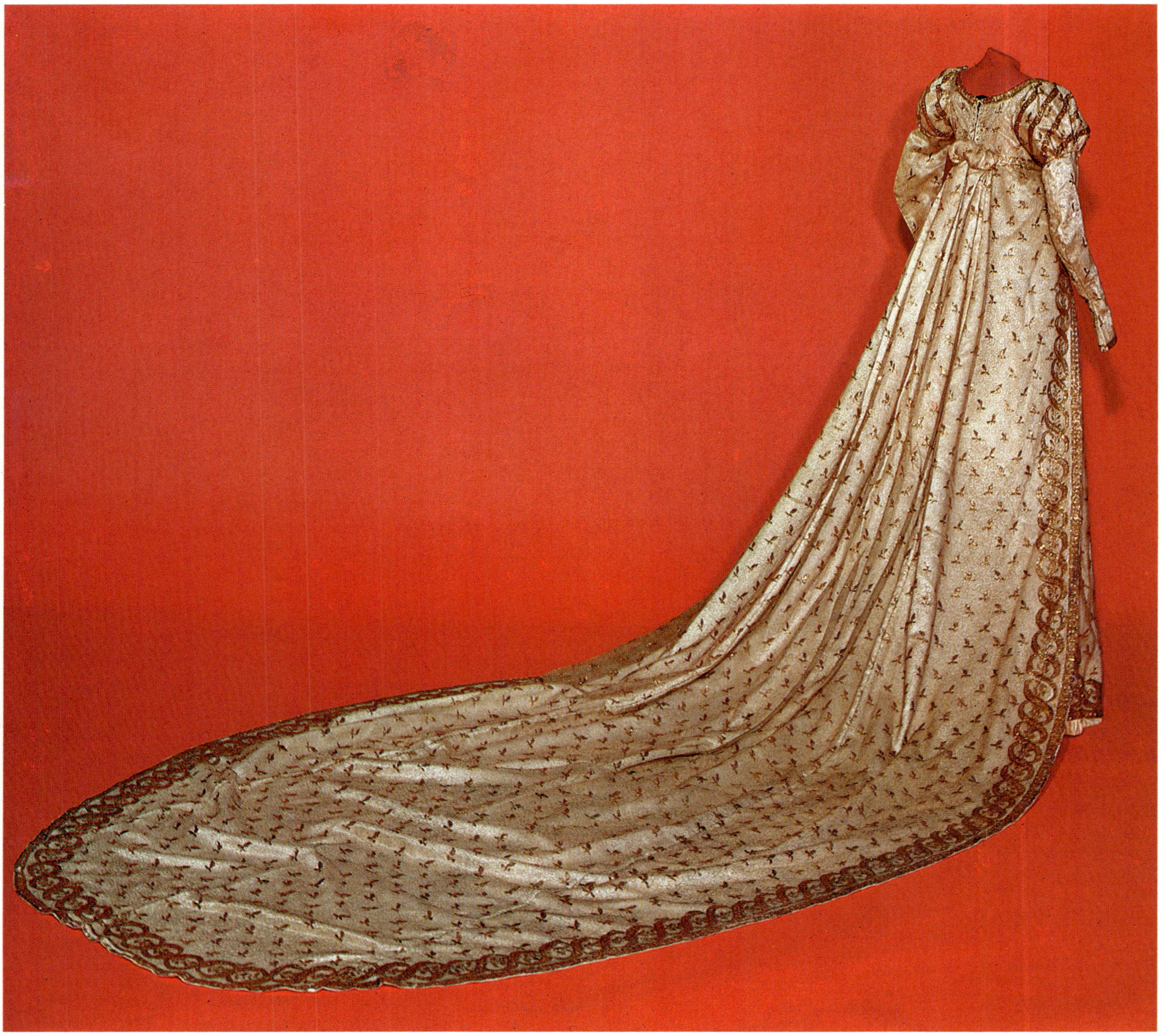

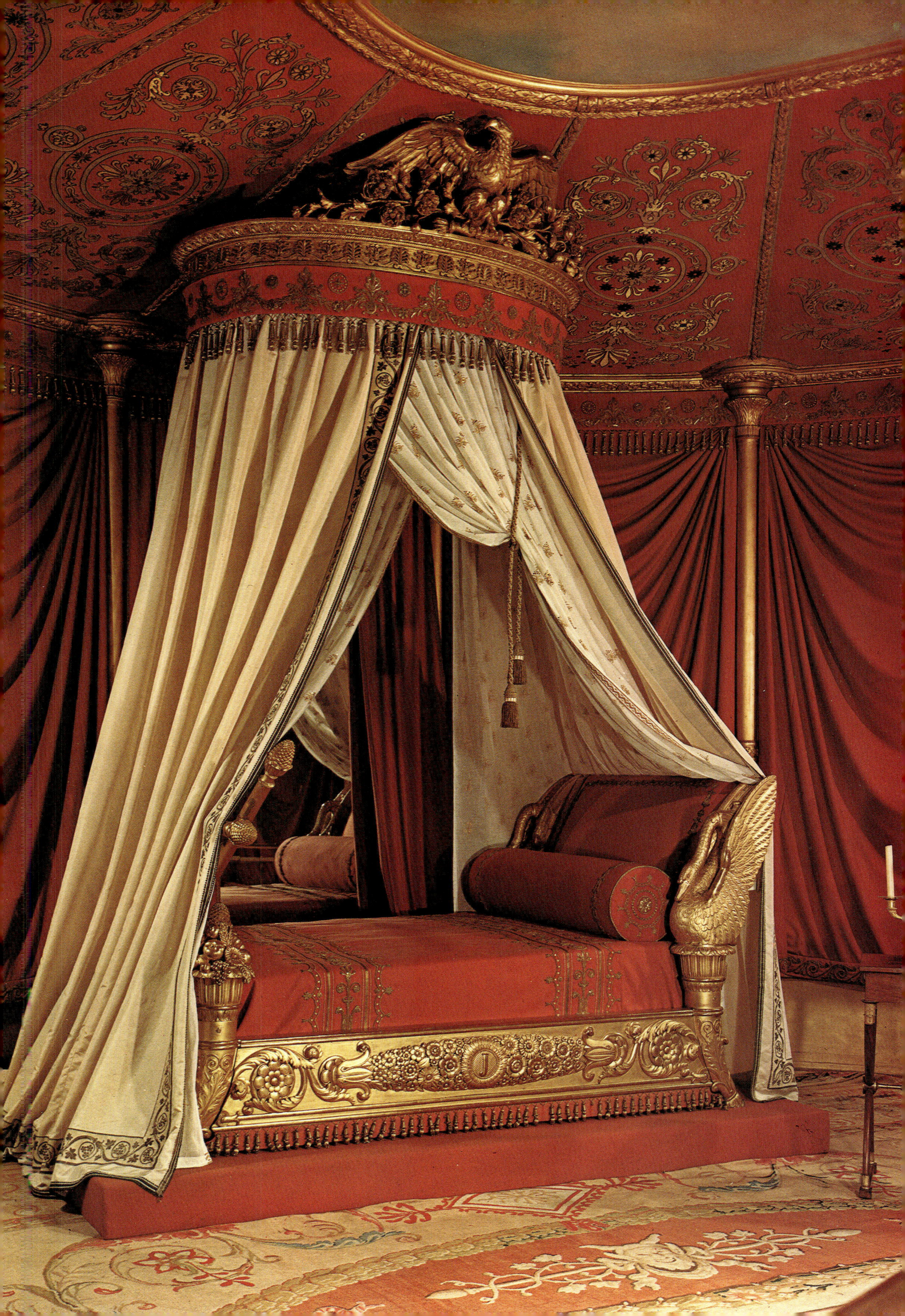

8_
A view of the Wardrobe, wit
glass-fronted cabinets arranged in th
former cupboards. Josephine's gowns
and court suits (that on the righ
belonged to the marquis d
Beauharnais, brother-in-law to th
Empress)

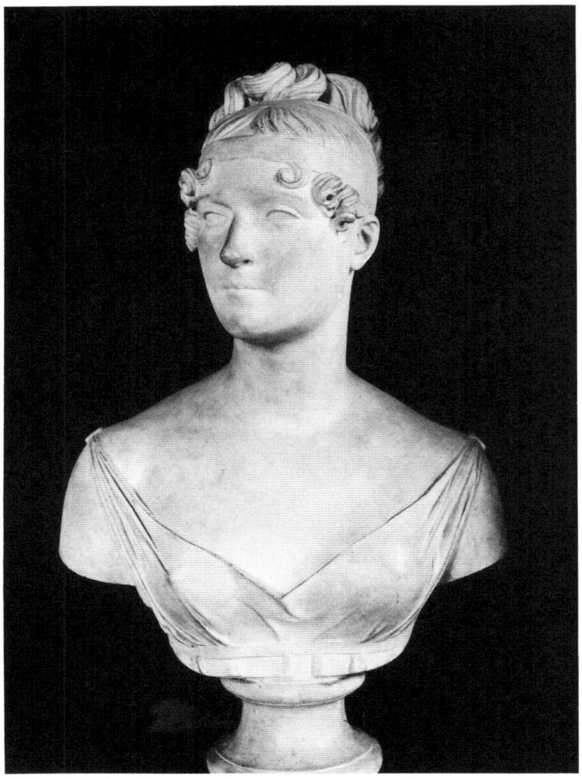

79
François-Joseph Bosio. Empress Josephine, bust, plaster, 1809 (gift Edward Tuck).

80
Bed-table with monogram JB (Josephine Bonaparte) comprising a toilet-set and a writing-set. Mahogany, silver, silver-gilt, ivory. About 1800.
By Martin-Guillaume Biennais (1764-1843).

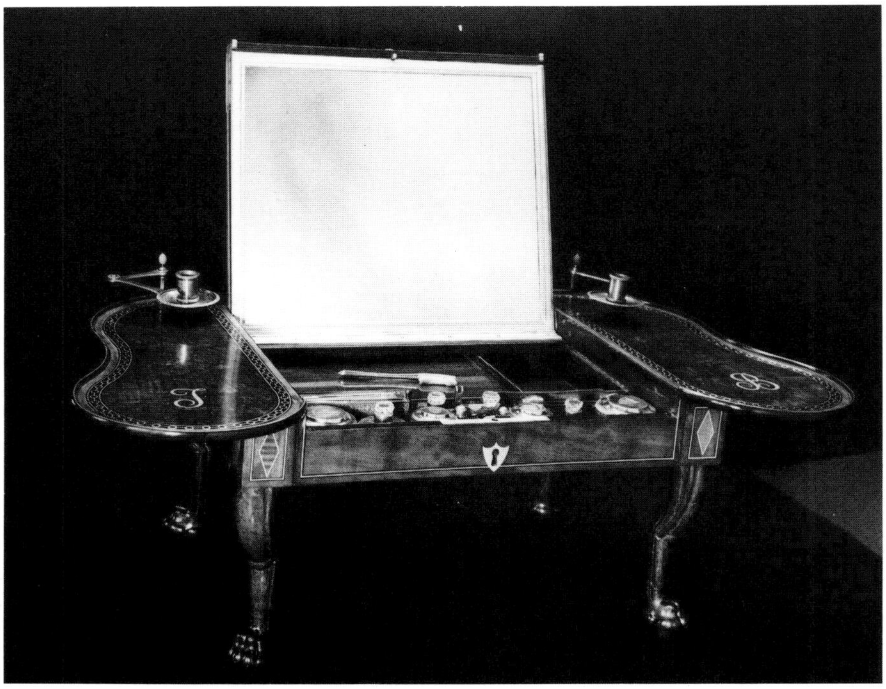

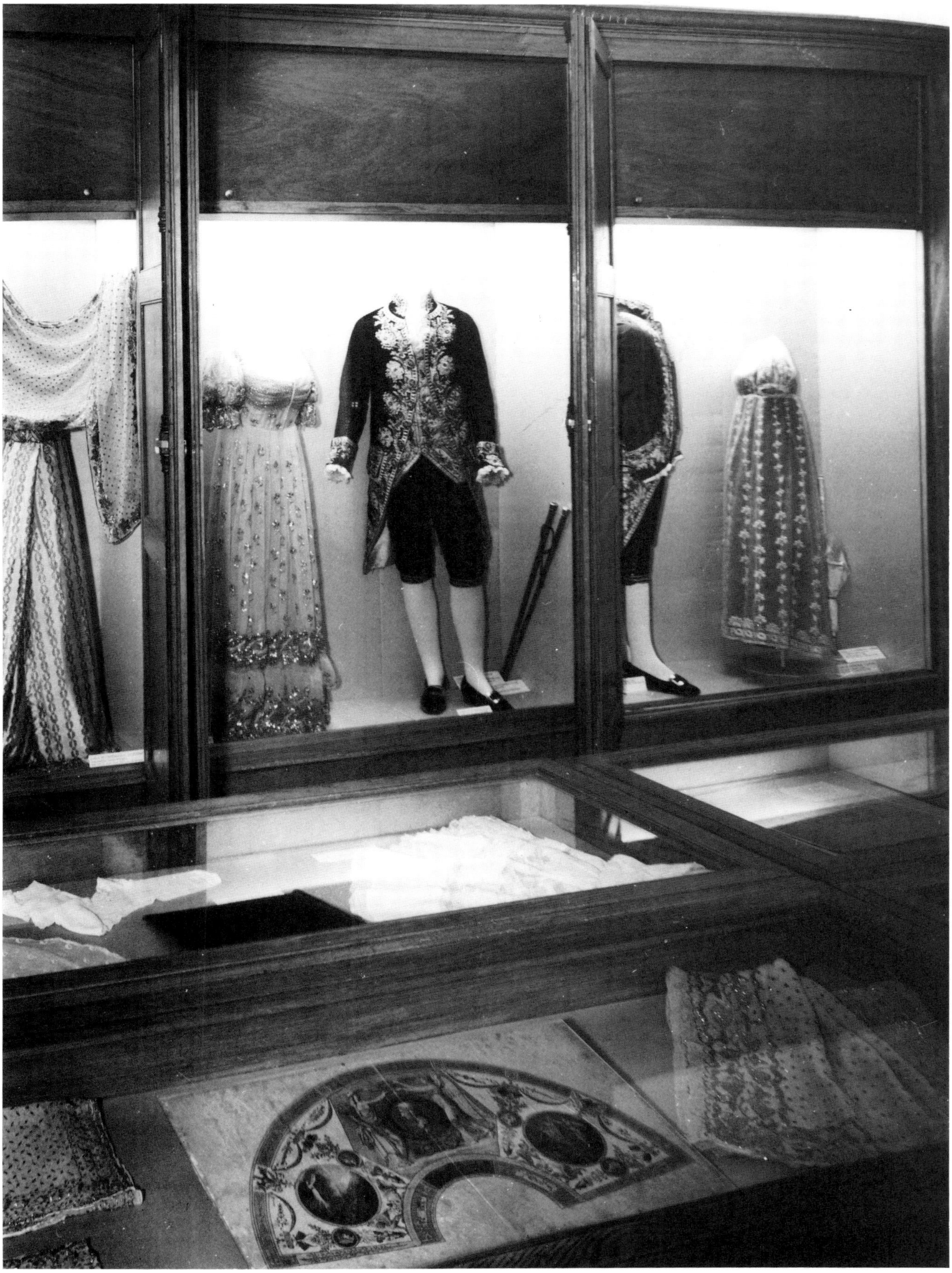

82
The Austerlitz', or Marshals' table. Sèvres porcelaine and gilt bronzes. Commissioned by the Emperor in 1806, executed 1808-1810 from a design by Percier. Portraits by Isabey, victories in biscuitware by Gérard, bronzes by Thomire, gold-work by Boullemier, Philippine and Moreau (gift Edward Tuck, 1929).

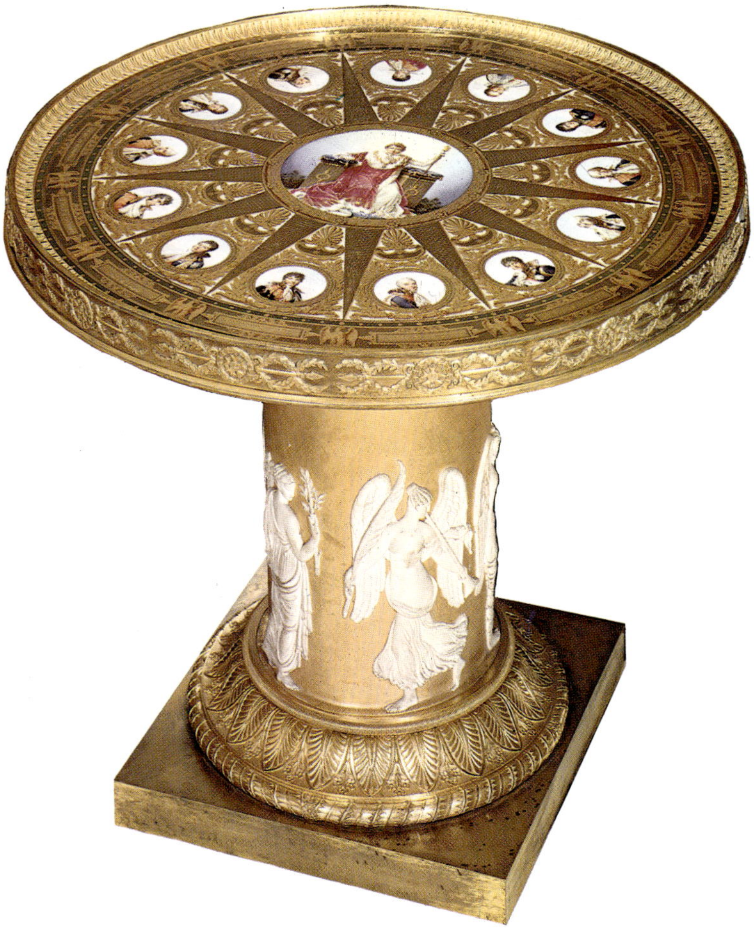

83
Room decorated with mythological frescoes painted in oil on plaster, from a small mansion in the rue Chantereine (rue de la Victoire) where Josephine and Bonaparte resided from 1796 to 1799 (gift of Princess George of Greece and Denmark, born Marie Bonaparte). *This room was formerly the site of Josephine's bathroom and a bedroom.*

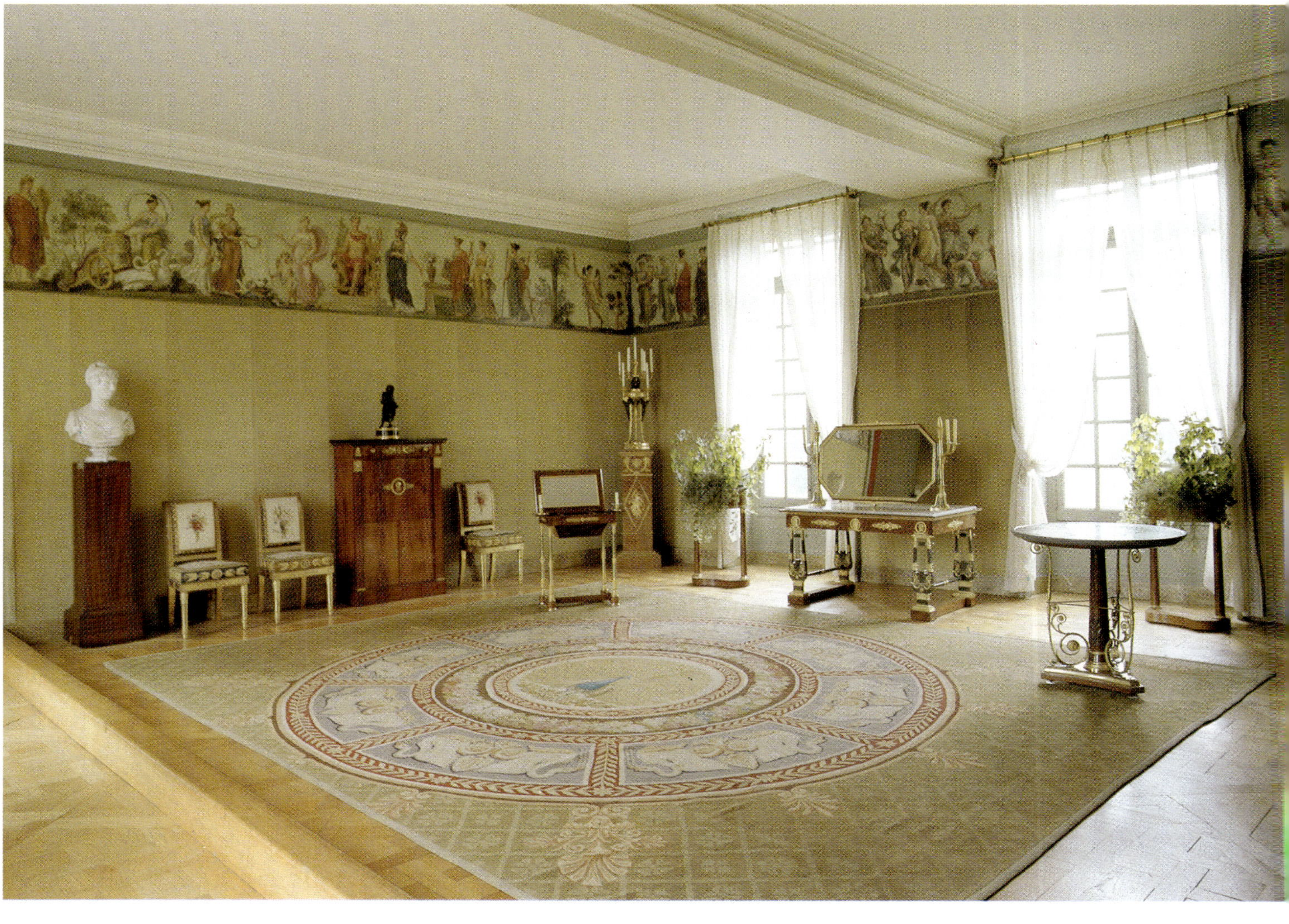

84
Jacques-Louis David (1784-1825).
Bonaparte crossing the Great Saint Bernard pass, signed "L. David, year IX" (1801-1802). The original of this painting, of which the artist himself made several copies
(bequest of Princess de la Moskowa, 1949).

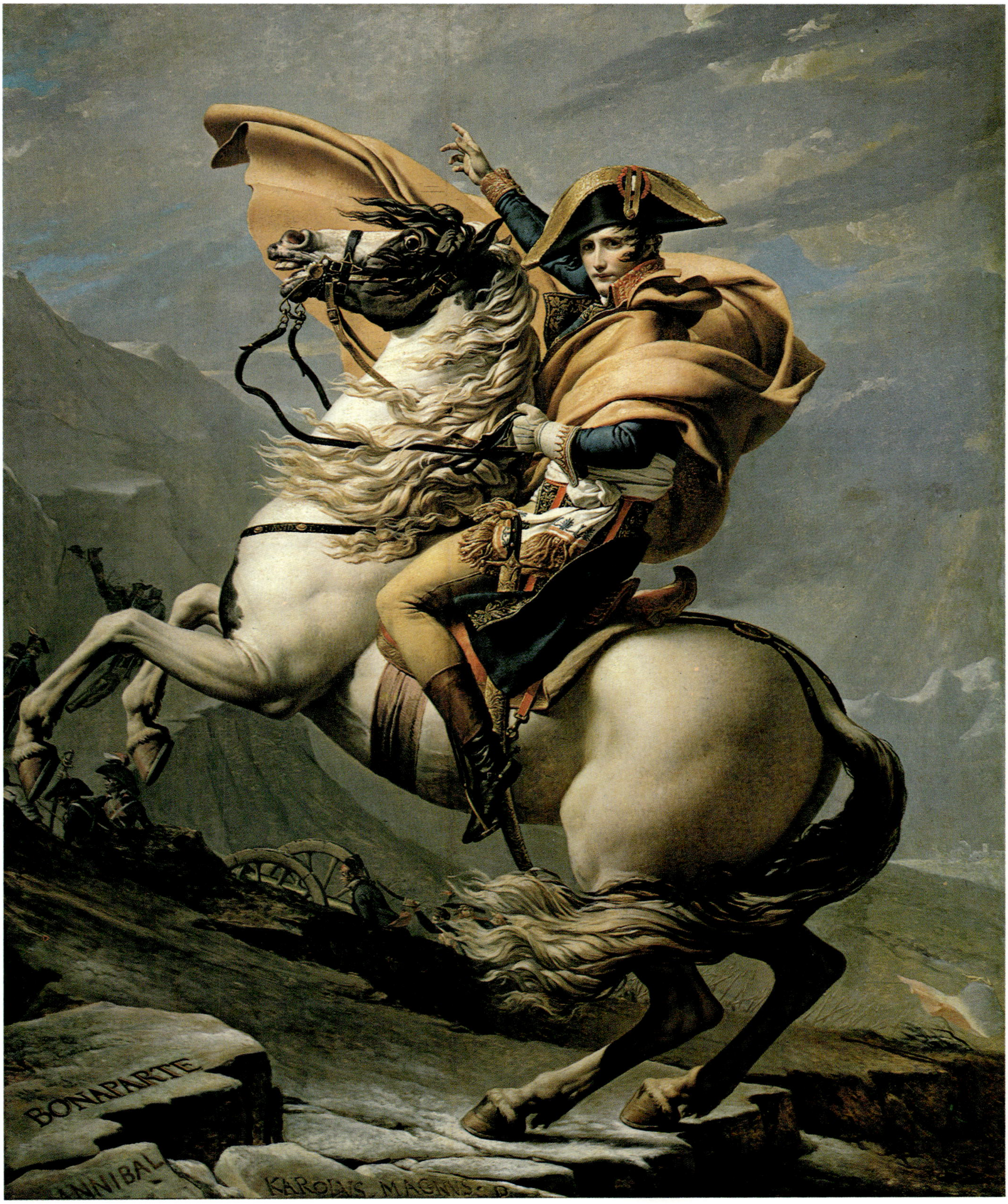

85
Claude Thiénon (1772-1846).
The Villa d'Este at Tivoli in 1802.
Josephine's former collection at Malmaison).

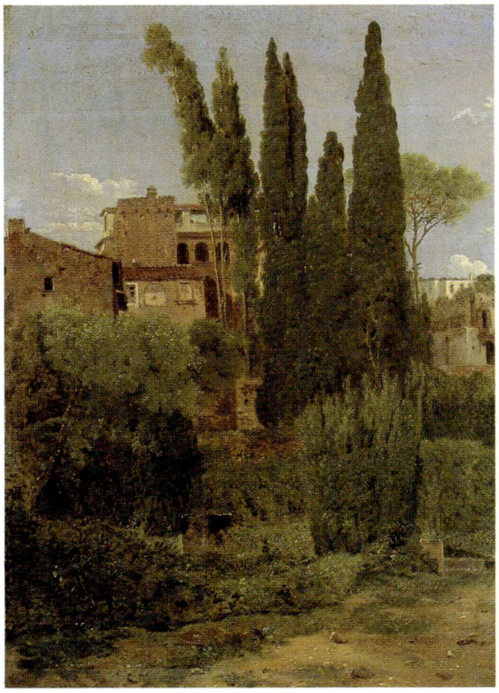

88
Jean-François Van Daël (1764-1840)
Julia's Tomb, oil on canvas, signed "Van Daël year XII", exhibited at the 1804 Salon. Josephine's former collection at Malmaison.

86
Henriette Lorimier.
Jeanne de Navarre.
Josephine's Former collection at Malmaison.

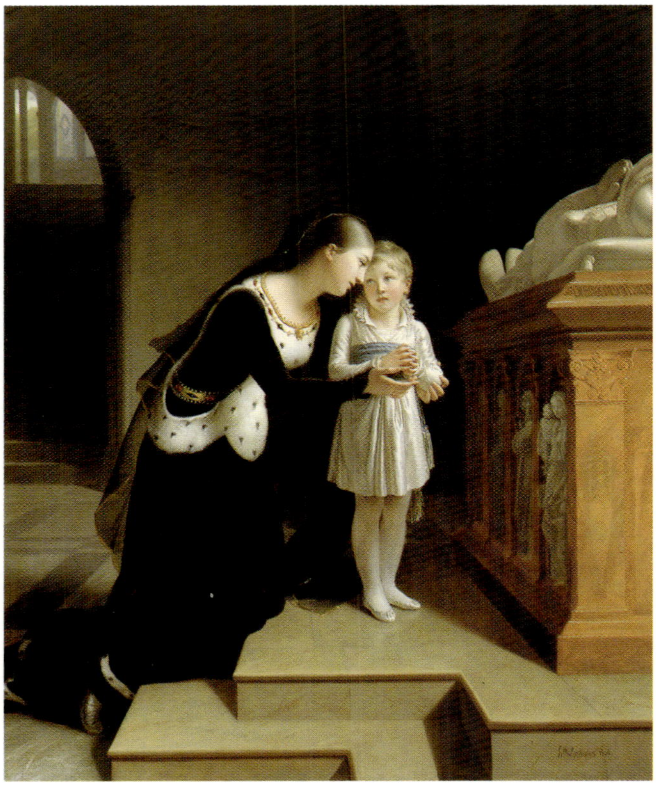

87
François-André Vincent.
Melancholy.
Josephine's Former collection at Malmaison.

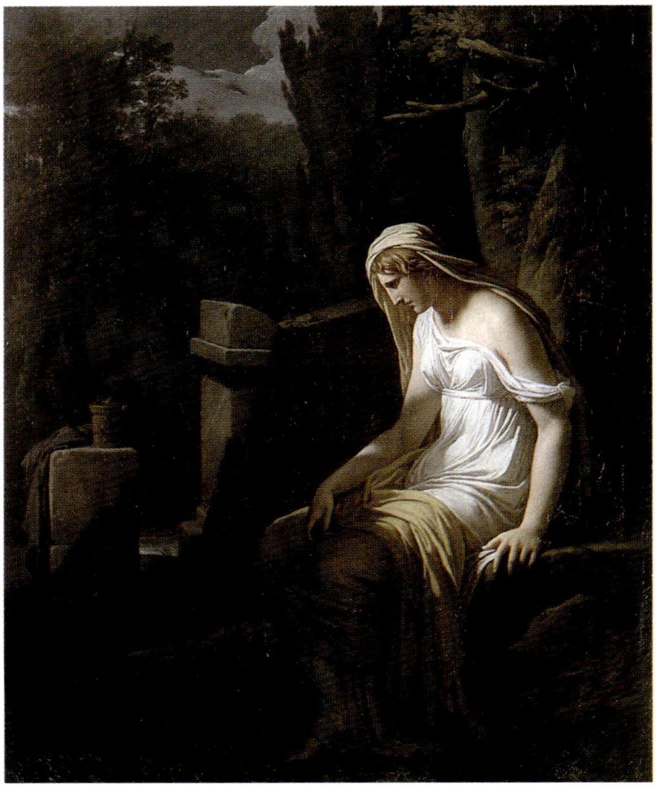

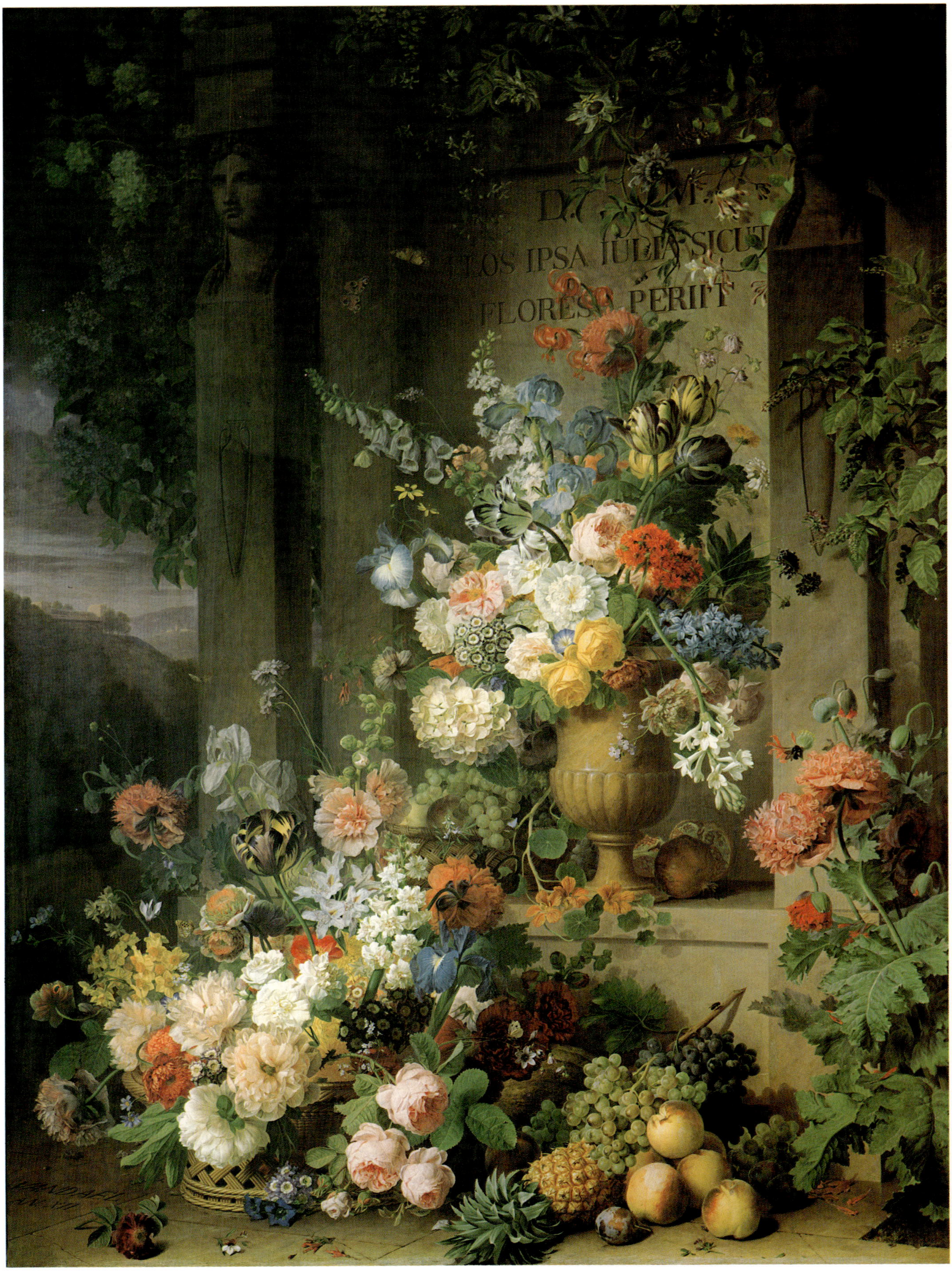
D. M.
FLOS IPSA IULIA SICUT
FLORES PERIIT

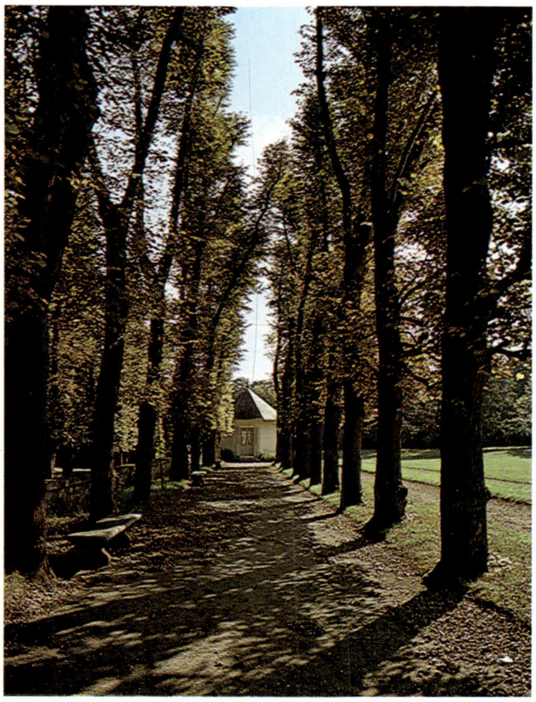

89-90
The Lime-tree Alley leading to the First Consul's Parilion.

In Spring.

In Autumn.

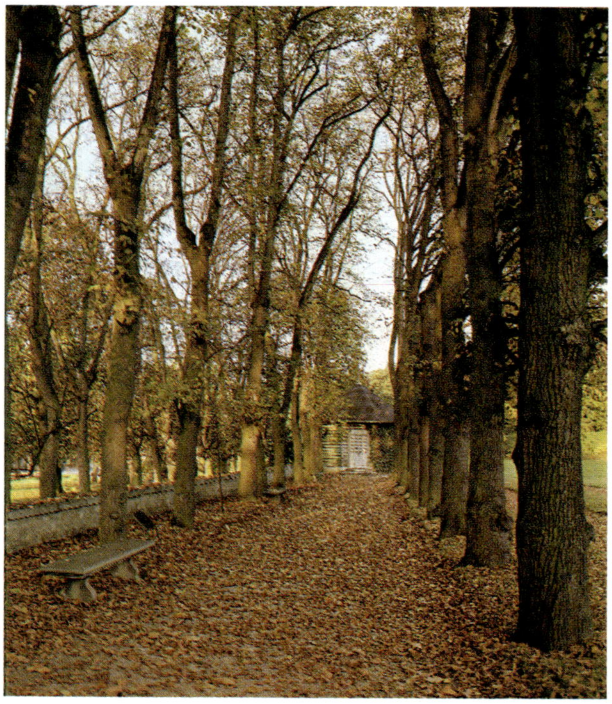

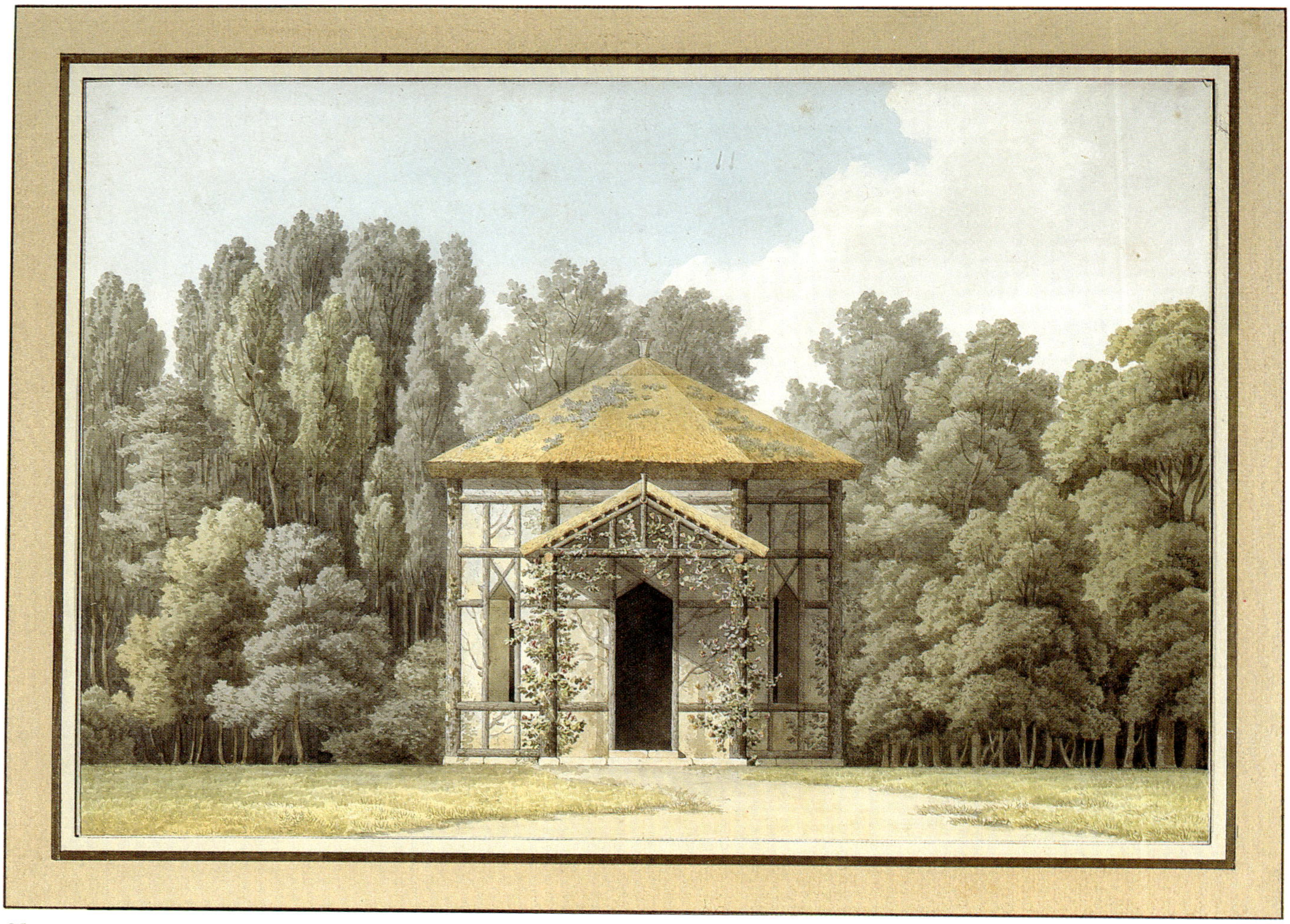

91
Louis-Hippolyte Lebas (1782-1867). The Malmaison Pavilion. Water-Colour.

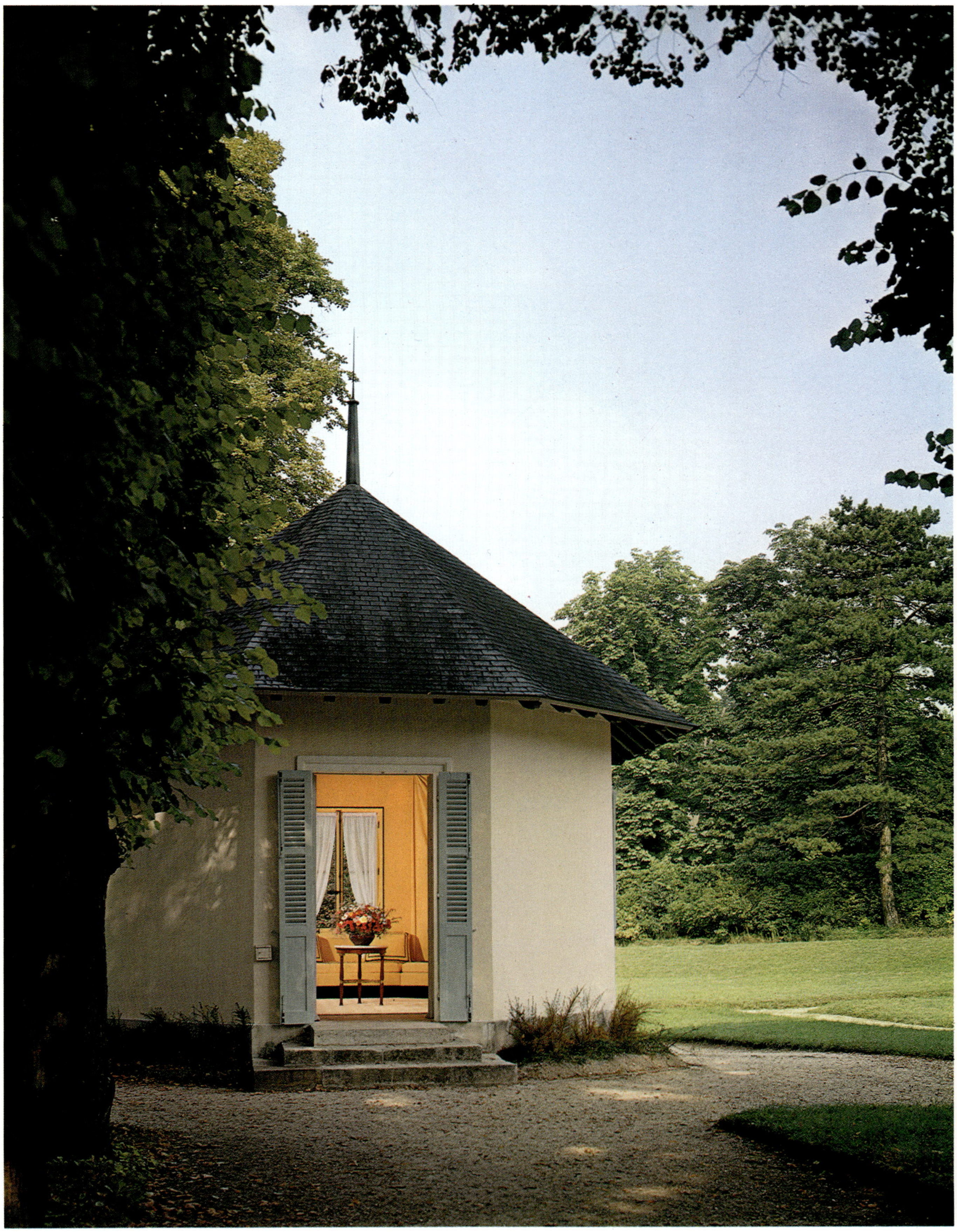

92
The Summer Pavilion, restored in conformance with the 1814 inventory.

93
Distant view of the château. On the left, a stele-fountain, formerly used as a stand for a marble relief by Girardon, "Melancholy", part of the Princess de Conti's tomb, brought to Malmaison in 1807. This sculpture is now in the Metropolitan Museum in New York.

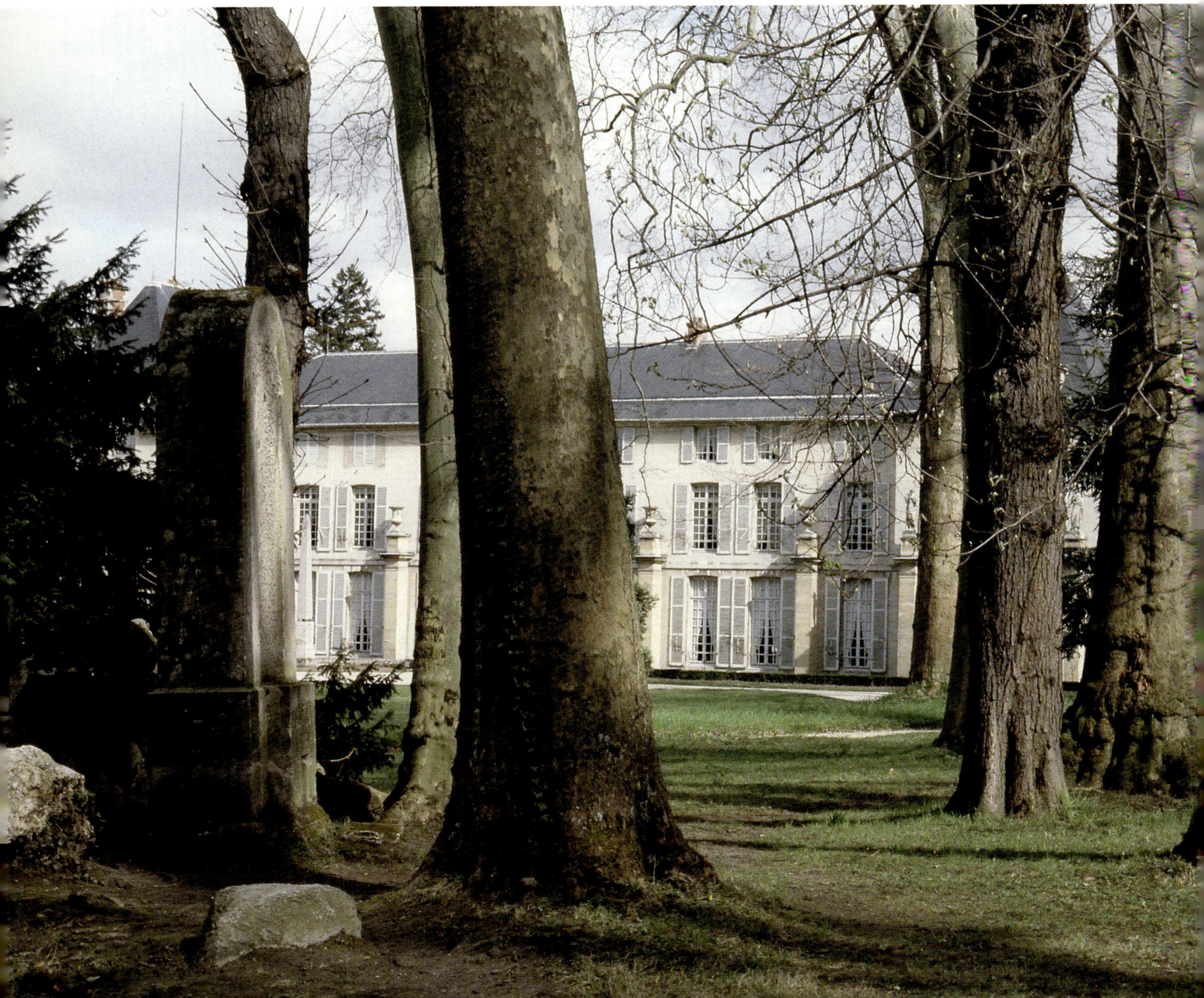

94
Berline-coach, delivered on June 12th 1812 by the coach-builders Cauyette and Getting for use by the Emperor. This carriage was specially fitted up and drove to Moscow and back. It was captured on the evening of June 18th 1815, after the defeat at Waterloo, by the Prussian army and presented to Field-Marshal Blücher (gift of Count Blücher von Wahlstatt, 1975).

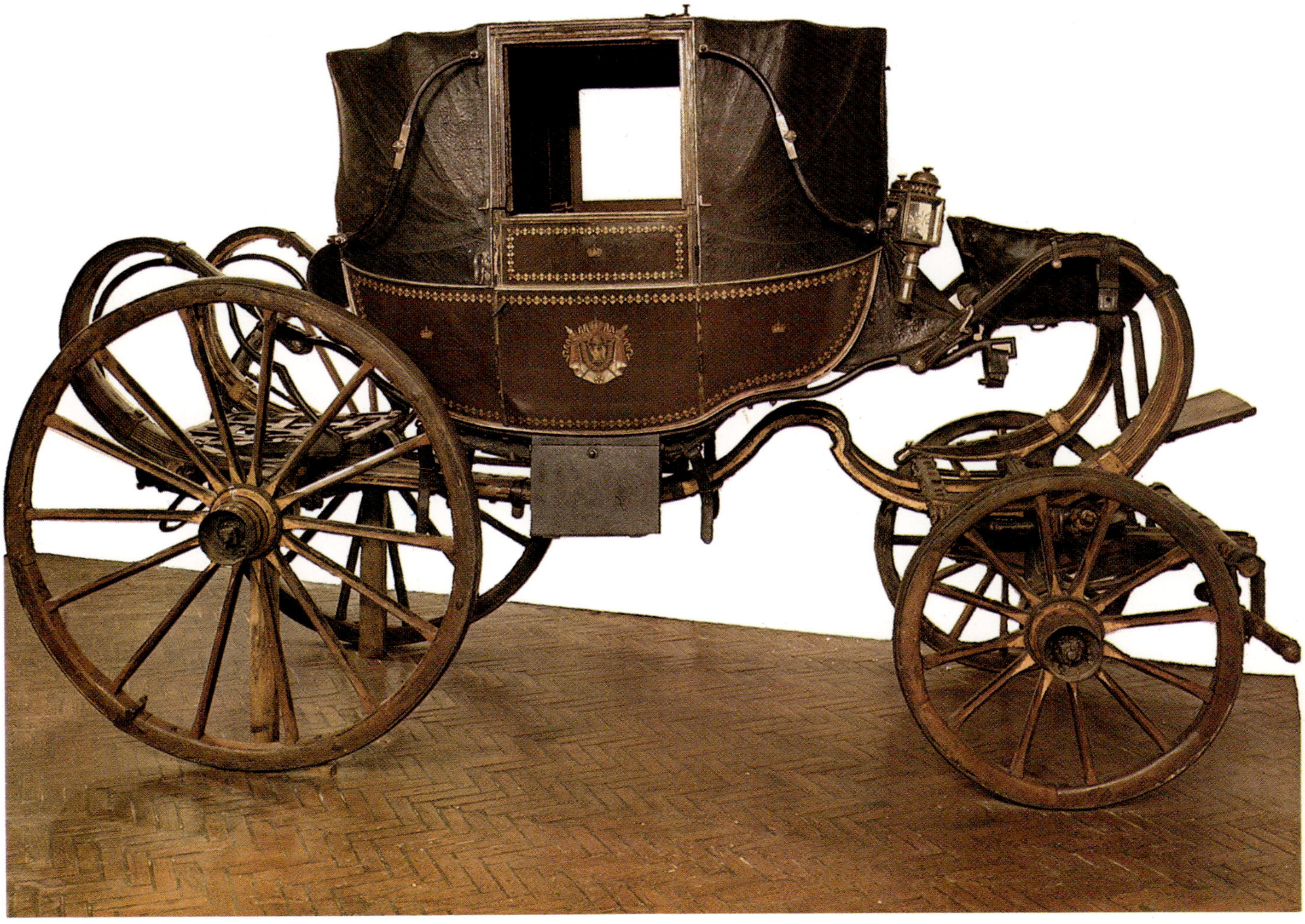

The owners of Malmaison
from the middle Ages to our days

Early XIIIth century
Hugues de Meulan or Meulent, Provost of Paris in 1196 († before 1244), and his wife Alice.

? - 1330
Onfroy de Cripatric, Scotsman (Kirk Patrick?) (†after 1334)

1330 - 31 October, 1339
Guy 1st de Châtres, abbot of St. Denis from 1326-1343 († 1350) by donation.

31 October, 1339-1341
Bureau of Charities of the Abbey of St. Denis, by donation.

1341 - ?
Robert de Lorris, Secretary to the King (†1380) and his wife Pernelle des Essars, by purchase.

1362 - ?
Agnes, countess of Acquise or Acquevise, widow of Thomas de la Marche, lord of Noueta or Monta, by purchase.

Before 1376
Nicolas de Chevreuse, equerry, bailliff-at-arms to the King, by purchase.

About 1376 - about 1380
Guy de Gouy, knight, lord of Falesque and Pontheaux († between 1377 and 1380) and Jeanne, his wife, by purchase.

About 1380 - 17 September, 1390
Louis de Gouy, equerry, his son, by inheritance.

21 September, 1390 - between Sepember and December 1400
Guillaume Goudet, bourgeois of Paris, sergeant-at-arms to Charles VI († 1400) then his widow Marie, by inheritance.

September-December 1400 - after 1414
Agnès Goudet, their daughter, and Jean Dubois, her husband, notary at the Châtelet in Paris, by inheritance.

1414 - about 1420
Malmaison seized in favour of the Abbey of St. Denis

About 1420 - 20 March, 1478
Marie Dubois, daughter of Jean Dubois, and Jean Dauvergne the elder, Master of Butchers in Paris († 1478), her husband, by inheritance.

20 March, 1478 - about 1505
Hugues Dauvergne, his son, butcher at the Master-Butchers of Paris († between 1504 and 1517) and his wife Robine Mignon, by inheritance.

About 1505 - 1561
Claude Dauvergne, equerry, his son, butcher at the Master-Butchers of Paris († 1561), by inheritance.

1561 - 14 December, 1596
Claude Perrot, his grandson, president of the Court of Enquiry of the Châlons Parliament († 1596) and his wife Catherine Croquet, by inheritance. He was the son of Jean Perrot, lord of Neuville-en Hez and of Marie Dauvergne, herself a daughter of Claude Dauvergne.

14 December, 1596 - 1 April, 1641
Christophe Perrot, his son, Provost of the Merchants of Paris (1573-1641) and his wife Jeanne Maynard († 1640), by inheritance.

1 April, 1641 - July, 1685
Charles Perrot, his son, Councillor to Parliament (1609-1685) and his wife Françoise de Laubespin († 1642), by inheritance.
Christophe Perrot had given the fief of Malmaison to his son Charles on the occasion of his marriage on January 14th 1635.

July, 1685 - 13 August, 1713
Marie-Madeleine Perrot, his daughter (1640-1713) wife by her first marriage of Jacques-Honoré Barentin, President of the Grand Council (1628-1689), then by her second marriage of Louis de Damas, lord of Cormaillon (about 1668-1692), by inheritance.
On October 31st 1703, she donated the domain to her son, but kept the usufruct; he died before her.

13 August, 1713 - 9 June, 1762
Charles-Amable-Honoré Barentin, Intendant of Orleans, his grandson (1703-1762) and his wife Marie-Catherine Lefèvre d'Ormesson (1706-1770),

by inheritance.
He was the son of Charles-Honoré Barentin (son of Marie-Madeleine Perrot) and Marie-Reine de Montchal.

9 June, 1762 - 24 May, 1763
Charles-Louis-François-de-Paule Barentin, his son (1736-1819).

24 May, 1763 - 31 December, 1764
Henri-François-de-Paule d'Aguesseau (1698-1764), second nephew of the last owner, by purchase.

31 December, 1764 - 23 March, 1771
His wife Françoise-Marthe-Angélique de Nollent (1704-1784), by inheritance.

23 March, 1771 - 21 April, 1799
Jacques-Jean Le Couteulx, lord du Molay (1740-1823) and his wife Geneviève-Sophie Le Couteulx de la Noraye (1753-1801), by purchase.

21 April, 1799 - 29 May, 1814
Marie-Joseph-Rose Tascher de la Pagerie, wife of General Napoleon Bonaparte, First Consul then Emperor of the French, by purchase.

29 May, 1814 - 21 February, 1824
Eugène-Rose de Beauharnais, duke of Leuchtenberg (1781-1824) son of Josephine by her first marriage, by inheritance.

21 February, 1824 - 17 Septembre, 1828
His widow Augusta-Amalia-Luisa of Bavaria, dowager Duchess of Leuchtenberg (1788-1851) as guardian of their children.

17 September, 1828 - 4 November, 1839
Jonas-Philip Hagerman (1774-1839), by purchase.

4 November, 1829 - 7 May, 1842
His widow Lucrèce-Davidine-Célestine Frat (1800-1862), by inheritance.

7 May, 1842 - 15 April, 1861
Augustin-Fernando Muñoz y Sanchez, duke of Riansares (1808-1873) and his wife Maria-Christina-Fernanda of two Sicilies (1806-1873) Queen-Regent then dowager Queen of Spain, by purchase.

15 April, 1861 - 6 September, 1870
Napoleon III, Emperor of the French (1808-1873), by purchase.

6 September, 1870 - 6 November, 1877
The French State.

6 November, 1877 - 19 October, 1882
Paul-Émile Gautier and his wife Victorine-Claire-Elisabeth Schlesinger, by purchase.

19 October, 1882 - 14 April, 1892
Alphonse-Nicolas Crépinet, Government architect (1826-1892), by purchase.

14 April, 1892 - 29 April, 1895
Marie-Germanica Maheu, widow of Pierre-Jean-François-Rodolphe Lachaume, by inheritance Crépinet.

29 April, 1895 - 20 May, 1895
Marie-Rosine Suchet d'Albuféra (1856-1895) deaconess of the order of Saint-Anna of Bavaria, grand-daughter of Marshal Suchet, by purchase.

20 May, 1895 - 12 August, 1896
Raoul-Napoléon Suchet, 3rd duke of Albuféra (1845-1925), her brother, and Isabelle-Marie David Suchet d'Albuféra (1847-1933), widow of Guy du Val, marquis de Bonneval, her sister, by inheritance.

12 August, 1896 - 25 January, 1904
Daniel Iffla Osiris (1828-1907), by purchase.

25 January, 1904
The French State accepts the donation of the château.

Bibliography

– B. Chevallier, *Malmaison, château et domaine des origines à 1904*, Paris, 1989.
– G. et N. Hubert, *Châteaux de Malmaison et de Bois-Préau.* Guide, Paris, 1986.

Crédits photographiques :

Photographies Studio Laverton, Rueil, à l'exception des numéros 8, 66, 71, 85, 86, 87, 89, 90, 91 (RMN), 11, 55, 83 (Arnaudet-RMN), 54, 61 (Schormans-Arnaudet-RMN), 17, 32, 38, 39 (Chevojon), 30 (La Rochelle, Museum d'histoire naturelle), 26 (Laboratoire des Musées nationaux), 1, 95 (Atelier Philippe Gentil), 68, 93 (Pougetoux), 73 (Giraudon).

Cet ouvrage a été achevé d'imprimer en juillet 1989
sur les presses de l'Imprimerie Moderne du Lion
d'après les maquettes de Philippe Gentil.
Dépôt légal : juillet 1989

Cover :
95
The Château : detail of the West façade :
the store bridge and its ornamentation.